Ninety-nine Novels

Ninety-nine Novels

The Best in English since 1939

A PERSONAL CHOICE BY

Anthony Burgess

Allison & Busby
LONDON

First published 1984 by
Allison & Busby Limited
6a Noel Street, London W1V 3RB
Reprinted 1984

British Library Cataloguing in Publication Data

Burgess, Anthony
Ninety-nine novels.
1. English fiction — 20th century
— History and criticism
I. Title
823'.912'09 PR881

ISBN 0-85031-584-0
ISBN 0-85031-585-9 Pbk

Set in 10/11 Palatino by
Falcon Graphic Art Ltd.,
Wallington, Surrey.
Printed and bound in Great Britain by
Richard Clay (The Chaucer Press)
Bungay, Suffolk.

CONTENTS

INTRODUCTION

1984 has arrived, but Orwell's glum prophecy has not been fulfilled. Some of us half-feared that, on the morning of January 1, we would wake with our seasonal hangovers to see Ingsoc posters on the walls, the helicopters of the Thought Police hovering, and our television sets looking at us. For thirty-five years a mere novel, an artifact meant primarily for diversion, has been scaring the pants off us all. Evidently the novel is a powerful literary form which is capable of reaching out into the real world and modifying it. It is a form which even the non-literary had better take seriously.

This seems a good moment to look back upon what has been done in the novel over the past forty-five years. Why not wait for the round fifty? Because it is more poetic to begin with the beginning of a world war and to end with the non-fulfilment of a nightmare. How far has the novel in English reflected the period accurately? How far has it opened our eyes to the future? How much entertainment has it given?

In this prefatory note I must deal, as briefly as I can, with problems of definition and aesthetic assessment. Before I ask what makes a good novel, I must ask what makes a novel at all. A novel, we know, is a work of fiction, but so is a short story, so is an anecdote or a blue comedian's joke. The shortest piece of science fiction ever written is: "That morning the sun rose in the west." But a true novel is an extended piece of fiction: length is clearly one of its parameters. You can expand a short story into a novella, a novella into a novel, but where is the dividing line? A novel can be as long as one thousand pages (expand that to more than three thousand: don't forget Proust) or as brief as a hundred. But if a hundred why not ninety? Why not fifty, forty? The only possible answer is a shrug.

But wait — the practical answer is provided by the

publishers, printers and binders who process a manuscript into printed copy dressed in an overcoat. If a work of fiction can be bound in hard covers, its pages stitched and not stapled (as a pamphlet is), we had better accept that it is a novel. This is a matter of convention only: it would be possible to publish a novel in the format of *The Times*. Indeed, I once had the notion of writing a fiction of a dying man who sees the unfolded *Times* on his bed and deliriously traces all his past life as though it were the content of that newspaper — news items, editorials, crossword puzzle, everything. If I did not write that book it is because the novel is a commercial form that is not intended to lose money.

Soon we may get our novels on floppy discs. Already I receive recorded readings of my novels intended for the blind. As, having begun my career as a kind of musician, I think of the novel as an auditory form, I am happy to listen to my work vibrating through the dark. But at this moment in history I have to accept, with everyone else, that a novel is a visual experience — black marks on a white page, many of these bound into a thickish book with a stiff cloth cover and an illustrative dust-jacket. Its paperback version is a poor but necessary thing, a concession to the pocket, the sickly child of the original. When we think of *War and Peace* or *David Copperfield* we see a fat spine with gold lettering, the guardian of a great potentiality (signs turned into sense), proudly upright on a shelf. BOOK can be taken as an acronym standing for Box of Organized Knowledge. The book called a novel is a box from which characters and events are waiting to emerge at the raising of the lid. It is a solidity, a paperback is a ghost.

There are more novels published than the average reader can possibly realize. There are even more — many more — novels submitted to publishers and unpublished. When I first began to write fiction I had little idea of the competition I was facing. I began to see, physically, the spate of fiction in English when I started to review novels for the *Yorkshire Post* in 1960. I received by mail all the current fiction. I lived in an East Sussex village at the time, and the local post office had to take on extra staff to cope with the flood of book-parcels. I was paid little for my fortnightly reviews, but every other Monday I was able to stagger to the railway station with two big book-crammed suitcases and take the train to Charing Cross and then a taxi to L. Simmonds on Fleet Street, there to sell all my review copies (except the few I wished to keep) at half the retail price. The banknotes I received were new and crisp and undeclarable to the Inland Revenue. They paid for the groceries and the odd bottle of cognac. This was the real reward of reviewing. Every other Monday, seeing me trudge to the train with my loads, the villagers would say: "There he goes, leaving his wife again." In fact, this was one way of keeping my wife, and myself.

When I opened my packages, it was clear that certain novels had to be reviewed whether I wished to review them or not. A new Graham Greene or Evelyn Waugh — this was the known brand-name which would grant an expected satisfaction. But the unknown had to be considered as well, unless they were published by Mills and Boon or Alvin Redman. After all, both Greene and Waugh produced first novels. V.S. Naipaul's first novel went totally unreviewed. The reviewer has a responsibility at least to dip into everything he is sent, and this is a reflection of the responsibility of the literary editor who does the sending. It is dangerous to ignore anything that is not clearly an ill-written bodice-ripper for a half-literate audience; even a bestseller like *Princess Daisy* demands consideration so that one may discover what makes it a bestseller. In my time I have read a lot of novels in the way of duty; I have read a great number for pleasure as well. I am, I think, qualified to compile a list like the one that awaits you a few pages ahead. The ninety-nine novels I have chosen I have chosen with some, though not with total, confidence. Reading pleasure has not been the sole criterion. I have concentrated mainly on works which have brought something new — in technique or view of the world — to the form. If there is a great deal of known excellence not represented here, that is because 99 is a comparatively low number. The reader can decide on his own hundredth. He may even choose one of my own novels.

When I say that I have read a great number of novels for sheer pleasure, as opposed to cold-eyed professional assessment, I have to admit that some of these novels never stood a chance of being placed in my list. I am an avid reader of Irving Wallace, Arthur Hailey, Frederick Forsyth, Ken Follett and other practitioners of well-wrought sensational fiction. The authors themselves do not expect considered reviews or academic theses, though, as I know, they are happy when they receive a kind word in a serious periodical. They do not pretend to be Henry James; they expect, unlike James, to make money out of a popular commodity. The fashioning of the commodity entails the jettisoning of certain elements which are essential to what is known as the serious or art novel — prose which essays effects beyond the mere conveying of basic information, complex psychology, narrative which is generated by the clash of character or of ideas. The popular novel of our day provides much technological information; it often depends on research more than insight; its clashes are physical; its character interest is minimal.

Professor Leslie Fiedler, of the University of New York at Buffalo, recently published a book called *What Was Literature?*, in which he seems to say that the study of the art novel (Joyce, James, Edith Wharton, Dorothy Richardson, Musil, Mann) is an outmoded discipline; that there is something wrong with our approach to reading if we cannot accommodate the spy novel, the pornographic fantasy, the comic strip. I am inclined to agree with him and to justify my own pleasure in the kind of book that is not represented in my list by referring to a new set of subliterary criteria that has not yet been formulated. We have to judge *The Day of the Jackal* or *The Crash of '79* by standards which neglect the Jamesian desiderata and make judgements in terms of the author's capacity for fulfilling the known expectations of the reader. Is this climax managed well? Is this technical information given with clarity? Are these characters sufficiently uninteresting not to interfere with the movement of the plot? Is this a *good read* for an invalid with a short attention-span whose head is muzzy with medicine?

Professors of literature neglect certain works because they perform their declared function (to entertain) all too thoroughly. There is nothing to discuss, there are no symbols to dig out, no ambiguities to resolve. It often seems to me that literature departments in universities depend on a certain *inefficiency* of technique in the works they set for study. In *The Mill on the Floss* the final flood is somewhat cursorily presented. Good, this means that the flood is purely symbolic and Floss clearly means *Fluss* or flux: George Eliot studied German philosophy. *Ulysses* and *Finnegans Wake* are studied because they contain difficulties: a professor can spend his life on unknotting the problems that Joyce probably sardonically knotted for the professor's benefit. If *Ulysses* succeeds as a novel, it may well be in spite of the wilful obfuscations that gained the professor his doctorate. A novel is primarily a presentation of human beings in action. The difference between the so-called art novel and the popular variety is perhaps that in the first the human beings are more important than the action and in the second it is the other way about.

I believe that the primary substance I have considered in making my selection is human character. It is the Godlike task of the novelist to create human beings whom we accept as living creatures filled with complexities and armed with free will. This free will causes trouble for the novelist who sees himself as a kind of small God of the

Calvinists, able to predict what is going to happen on the final page. No novelist who has created a credible personage can ever be quite sure what that personage will do. Create your characters, give them a time and place to exist in, and leave the plot to them; the imposing of action on them is very difficult, since action must spring out of the temperament with which you have endowed them. At best there will be a compromise between the narrative line you have dreamed up and the course of action preferred by the characters. Finally, though, it must seem that action is there to illustrate character; it is character that counts.

The time and space which a fictional character inhabits ought to be exactly realized. This does not mean that an art novelist need, in the manner of the pop novelist, get all his details right. Frederick Forsyth would not dream of making Milan Airport (Linate) out of his skull, but Brian Moore, in his recent *Cold Heaven*, equips Nice Airport with a security check system which it does not possess. This is not a grave fault, since the rest of the Côte d'Azur is realized aromatically enough. Many novelists rightly consider human probability more important than background exactitude. It often happens that a created background, like Graham Greene's West Africa in *The Heart of the Matter*, is more magical than the real thing. It is the spatio-temporal extension of character that is more important than public time and location — the hair on the legs, the aching eyetooth, the phlegm in the voice. It is not enough for a novelist to fabricate a human soul: there must be a body as well, and an immediate space-time continuum for that body to rest or move in.

The management of dialogue is important. There is a certain skill in making speech lifelike without its being a mere transcription from a tape recorder. Such a transcription never reads like fictional speech, which is artful and more economical than it appears. One could forgive Denis Wheatley, who wrote well-researched novels of the occult, a good deal if only his characters sounded like people. There is too much, in the novels of Arthur Hailey and Irving Wallace, of the pouring out of information cribbed directly from an encyclopaedia as a substitute for real speech. The better novelists write with their ears.

A good novel ought to have a shape. Pop novelists never fail to gather their strands of action into a climax: they are helped in this by the comparative inertness of their characters. The characters of an art novel resist the structure which their creators try to impose on them; they want to go their own way. They do not even want the book to come to an end and so they have, sometimes arbitrarily, as in E.M. Forster, to be killed off. A good novel contrives, nevertheless, somehow to trace a parabola. It is not merely a slice of life. It is life delicately moulded into a shape. A picture has a frame and a novel ends where it has to — in some kind of resolution of thought or action which satisfies as the end of a symphony satisfies.

I now tread dangerous ground. A novel ought to leave in the reader's mind a sort of philosophical residue. A view of life has been indirectly propounded that seems new, even surprising. The novelist has not preached: the didactic has no place in good fiction. But he has clarified some aspect of private or public morality that was never so clear before. As novels are about the ways in which human beings behave, they tend to imply a judgement of behaviour, which means that the novel is what the symphony or painting or sculpture is not — namely, a form steeped in morality. The first English novels — *Clarissa Harlowe* and *Pamela* by Samuel Richardson — were highly moral. We still cannot prevent a moral attitude from creeping into our purely aesthetic assessment of a book. Oscar Wilde, who said that to write immorally could only mean to write badly, nevertheless produced in *The Picture of Dorian Gray* a black-and-white morality novel which almost preaches a Sunday sermon. It is easy to escape the origins of the novel as a moral tract disguised as entertainment. Oscar Wilde's Miss Prism says of her own novel that the good end well and the bad end badly: "that is why it is called fiction." To many readers of fiction, and not necessarily naive ones, there is profound dissatisfaction when the deeper morality is subverted. Leopold Bloom can masturbate without his nose dropping off, and Ann Veronica can break the sexual taboos, but very few fictional characters can kill — except in revenge — and get away with it. The strength of a novel, however, owes nothing to its confirmation of what conventional morality has already told us. Rather a novel will question convention and suggest to us that the making of moral judgements is difficult. This can be called the higher morality.

George Orwell, in his essay on Dickens, said that, with any author he found sympathetic, a portrait of the author seemed to rise from the page — not necessarily like the author as he really was but more the author as he ought to be. Orwell saw Dickens as a bearded man with a high colour, angry but laughing with the generosity of a ninteenth-century liberal. The implication here is that the personality of the novelist is important to us — the personality as revealed in his work and not in his private life (the private lives of many artists do not bear looking at). Some novelists, like Gustave Flaubert and James Joyce, have tried to obliterate themselves entirely from their fictions, seeking the anonymity of the divine creator, but they reveal themselves in style and imagery and cannot altogether hide their attitudes to their characters. It is clear that Joyce is on the side of Bloom, though he never intrudes to make a comment, as Thackeray and Dickens always did. The author is present with us on every page, sometimes, as with Somerset Maugham, as an idealised portrait ranking as a character — rational, tolerant, travelled — though more often as the man whose heavy breathing we can hear as he puts his words together. We have to *like* our author. It is hard to like Ms Marilyn French when she uses her fiction (as in *The Bleeding Heart*) to castrate innocent men; it is very hard indeed to like Harold Robbins, who evidently loves violence while pretending to hate it. It is not easy to love Judith Krantz, who, on the evidence of *Princess Daisy*, has never read a philosopher or heard Beethoven and imposes on her personages a like cultural nullity. It is hard to like an author who knows too much and shows off.

We do not demand of an author that he be an intellectual (though my own temperament prefers Johnson's *Rasselas* to Jane Austen's *Sense and Sensibility*, something I can do little about), but we have a right to intelligence, a knowledge of the human soul, a certain decency — quite apart from professional skill. Probably this imputation of decency is important: all the great novels have been about people trying to be kinder, more tolerant. Aldous Huxley concluded at the end of his hard-thinking life that all you could ask of people was that they try to be a little nicer. This does not mean that authors have to be nice to their characters. Geoffrey Firmin in *Under the Volcano* has a wretched time and ends by being killed and thrown like a dead dog down a ravine. But the way of tragedy is the way of arousing not only terror but pity. Some characters have to suffer to demonstrate the horror of life, but the author takes only a technical pleasure in delineating those sufferings. Novels are about the human condition, which is not easy, and how, if possible, to cope with it. The author is concerned about this, and he is concerned that you, the reader, be concerned.

As you start on my list, you will discover that few of these attributes seem to apply. *After Many a Summer* is bitter satire: where is the human concern? The concern seems negative: a desirable world for human beings defined in terms of what it is not. *At Swim-Two-Birds* is little more than a game. Henry Green tries to make a kind of novelistic poem out of the surface of life. *Finnegans Wake* is a comic nightmare. Later you will find Ivy Compton-

Burnett using most unrealistic language and showing an interest only in the structural consequences of sin. It is very hard indeed to devise universal parameters for the novel. The novel, one supposes, is about human life, but the French anti-novel (which, of course, cannot figure here) appears to deny even that: certainly Nathalie Sarraute will not accept the traditional view of the human personality as a unity. So do we end with some such definition as: a verbal construct in which invented human characters appear positively or negatively, act or do not act, speak or do not speak? I do not know. But I do know that we carry a scale of values whereby we know that *Anna Karenina* is a great novel and *The Carpetbaggers* an inferior one, and that our standards have something to do with the management of language and concern with the human personality. Sometimes the management of language will be so remarkable that we will be prepared to forgive the lack of human interest; sometimes character interest will condone verbal and structural incompetence. Judging a novel is a rule-of-thumb matter; we cannot appeal to any aesthetic tribunal which will lay down universal laws.

Anyway, all the novelists listed here have added something to our knowledge of the human condition (sleeping or waking), have managed language well, have clarified the motivations of action, and have sometimes expanded the bounds of imagination. And they entertain, or divert, which means to turn our faces away from the repetitive patterns of daily life and look at humanity and the world with a new interest and even joy. Though I have, with right modesty, excluded myself from my list, as a practising novelist I think I know my own aims, and I do not think these are very different from those of my colleagues in Britain, the Commonwealth and the United States. We want to entertain, surprise, and present the preoccupations of real human beings through invented ones.

I like to think of these novels, and all the other good ones that are not here, as products of a more or less common culture practised in the place called Anglophonia — the world where English is spoken. But, having mentioned above the national distributions of this language, it is in order to regret that some English-speaking countries have to be represented more than others. New Zealand, alas, is not featured at all; Canada appears only twice and Australia only once; the output is shared mainly by the British Isles and the United States. This cannot be helped. I would be delighted to see the Nobel Prize for Literature go to Canada or New Zealand, as it has already gone to Australia, but such considerations of Commonwealth pride are probably unworthy. It is the work that counts. You have here, then, brief accounts of ninety-nine fine novels produced between 1939 and now. There are, however, slightly fewer than ninety-nine fine novelists. Though most are featured once only, some appear twice, and Aldous Huxley three times. Some novels are *romans fleuve* or river novels in several volumes, but they are treated with little more ceremony than works of a hundred or so pages. The books are not arranged in order of merit but in order of date of publication. When more than one novel was published in the same year I have not observed a pedantic chronology involving month of publication: I have merely placed the authors in alphabetical order. The multi-volumed novels are dated according to the appearance of the first volume.

If you disagree violently with some of my choices I shall be pleased. We arrive at values only through dialectic.

A.B.
Monaco
1984

Party Going

HENRY GREEN [1939]

Green, whose real name was Yorke, was concerned with bringing to the novel-form a close-knit unity more appropriate to poetry than to fiction. The brevity of his titles indicates the economy of the works to which they are attached — *Blindness, Living, Caught, Back, Nothing, Concluding*. Green's experiences, after Eton and Oxford, in the Midlands factory owned by the Yorke family, led him to write, in *Living*, the best brief novel about factory life that we possess. The workers in the book are not statistics in an industrial report but people living their own lives. They are like the pigeons they keep in their lofts — homebound and yet free. These pigeons flutter and whirr throughout the novel as a unifying symbol.

One could choose any novel of Green's as a typical expression of his idiosyncratic talent. If I choose *Party Going* it is because the resonance of war which hums through it gives it, for me, a special poignancy. It looks like a piece of expressionist symbolism, but it has no message. Fog delays the departure of a boat-train, and the station hotel is filled with passengers indefinitely waiting — workers on the ground floor, rich young people in the rooms above. If this were an expressionistic play by, say, Ernst Toller, the workers would take over the whole hotel, but they do not — they merely sing. Only one memorably strange thing seems to happen: an old lady finds a dead pigeon on the station platform and she wraps it carefully in paper. What does this mean? It is perhaps merely an eccentric act impinging on the behaviour of social groups which offers no surprises. Or, if we wish, we can think of the dove of peace falling dead at our feet while the fog of war puts an end to party going or the going of parties on their travels. It does not much matter: the whole book is a carefully wrought poem, and if we try to extract a meaning the whole structure is in danger of collapsing. What does a Chopin nocturne mean? The same negative answer applies to all Green's novels.

After Many a Summer

ALDOUS HUXLEY [1939]

An American multimillionaire, Jo Stoyte, has everything that money can buy but little peace of mind. In his hideous Hearst-like castle in Southern California he broods on the approach of death and perdition. His shady financial successes exacerbate rather than mollify the fear of hell implanted by his Christian fundamentalist upbringing. He, like the young Jane Eyre, wants to put off hell as long as possible and so finances scientific research into longevity. But the secret of long life is found not in the laboratory but in an eighteenth-century nobleman's diary bought up in a job-lot library by Stoyte's British agent. The writer of the diary noted the longevity of the carp in his fishpond and sought to prolong his own life by eating their raw minced guts. In the spring of 1939, while Britain is preparing for war, he is found to be still alive along with his housekeeper, hidden in a cellar, surreptitiously fed by his descendants. The great secret has been discovered, but there is a snag: to live a couple of centuries you must reconcile yourself to reverting to the ape. Jo Stoyte, hearing animal squeals of sexual enjoyment, reflects that "they seem to be having a pretty good time".

Being a novel by Huxley, *After Many a Summer* (whose American title completes the Tennysonian line with *Dies the Swan*) is more than a grim satire on materialism, unenlightenment and related evils of the age. It contains, in the long monologues of Mr Propter, expositions of the Huxley philosophy of non-attachment; it is about sex and art and the possibilities and limitations of science. It is Huxleyan in that it is a novel with a brain, and if it nags at human stupidity when it should be getting on with the story — well, we accept the didacticism as an outflowing of the author's concern with the state of the modern world. Huxley's novels are always *concerned*, and therein lies their strength and continuing relevance.

Finnegans Wake

JAMES JOYCE [1939]

This long and difficult work represents for many the end of the period which began in 1922 with T.S. Eliot's *The Waste Land* and Joyce's own *Ulysses*. That was the age of Modernism — a movement in literature which rejected the late nineteenth-century concept of Liberal Man and presented (as in Ernest Hemingway and D.H. Lawrence) Natural Man, and (in Eliot, Joyce and, later, Evelyn Waugh and Graham Greene) Imperfect Man. To eliminate all traces of Victorian and Edwardian optimism, literary style had to change from the orotund to the spare, ironic, experimental. There was also a franker realism than known in the old days. The frank realism of *Ulysses* earned moral censure, and the experimental prose caused difficulties for the ordinary reader. These difficulties were, however, nothing in comparison with those to be encountered in *Finnegans Wake*.

While *Ulysses* is a book of the sunlight, depicting the events of an ordinary day in Dublin in 1904, *Finnegans Wake* is a work of the dark. It presents, with no concessions to waking sense, a dream in a specially invented dream language. The hero is a publican in Chapelizod, just outside Dublin, and, while his waking name is probably Mr Porter, his dream name is Humphrey Chimpden Earwicker. He has a wife, Ann, a daughter, Isabel, and twin sons named Kevin and Jerry. Earwicker is the eternal builder of cities, while his wife is all the rivers on which cities are built, but all cities become Dublin and all rivers flow into the Liffey. Isabel becomes the eternal temptress who brings great men low, and the twin boys become all the rival males of myth and history, from Cain and Abel to Jack Dempsey and Gene Tunney. Earwicker's long dream is really a mammoth comedy in which his household and the customers of his pub play all the rôles. The theme of the play is simple: the father is a builder, but his creative gift is an aspect of sexual sin (no erection without an erection). His sons are most typically presented as a poetic dreamer and a political demagogue. They fight to take over the rôle of their father, but, as each is only one half of the creative egg (Earwicker often appears as Humpty Dumpty, author of his own great fall), they lack the power and skill to depose him. The great paternal creator is thrust underground, but he always rises again. One of the parts he plays is that of the god-giant Finnegan, who, like Christ, may be killed and eaten and drunk but is indestructible. The action of the dream takes place in 1132 AD, a symbolic year which combines figures of falling and rising — bodies fall at the rate of 32 feet per second per second; when we have counted on our ten fingers we start again with the number 11. Meanwhile the wifely motherly river — who never dies — flows on quietly beneath the turbulent city which is her husband.

Some say that this fantasy is not really a novel. In that it has distinguishable characters — always changing their shapes and names but always brilliantly delineated — and that there is a summarizable plot and a fixed mise en scène — the master bedroom over the pub — it is difficult to deny that it belongs to the genre. We had to wait for the war in order to begin to understand it (it was in many an intellectual fighting man's kitbag), but it is the post-war age that has produced a horde of Joyce scholars dedicated to dragging it further into the light. Janus-faced, it looks back to the twenties but also to the indefinite future: no writer of the contemporary period has been able to ignore it, though most writers have succeeded in not being influenced by it.

At Swim-Two-Birds

FLANN O'BRIEN [1939]

Flann O'Brien was an Irish journalist, Gaelic scholar and dedicated drinker whose real name was Brian O'Nolan. Of his very few books, *The Hard Life* and *The Dalkey Archive* are slight but funny, and *The Third Policeman* is a vision of hell which does not quite come off, but *At Swim-Two-Birds* is probably a masterpiece. Philip Toynbee, the novelist and critic, once said: "If I were cultural dictator ... I would make *At Swim-Two-Birds* compulsory reading in all our universities." Joyce said of Flann O'Brien: "There's a real writer with the true comic spirit." This book owes something to Joyce, but this may mean merely that both Joyce and O'Brien were Irish.

The book is sometimes difficult, but it is no literary heavyweight. It is even, which Joyce's work is not, whimsical. The narrator is an Irish student who, when not lying in bed or pub-crawling, is writing a novel about a man named Trellis who is writing a book about his enemies who, in revenge, are writing a book about him. The book is a book about writing a book about writing a book. This is very modern (compare the Argentine Borges) in that it does not pretend that literature is reality. The student-narrator is interested not merely in literature but in Irish mythology, which enables him to bring in Finn MacCool (Joyce's Finnegan) and indulge in comic-heroic language which sounds as though it is translated from the Erse: "The knees and calves to him, swealed and swathed with soogawns and Thomond weed-ropes, were smutted with dungs and dirt-daubs...."

Flann O'Brien discovered a way of counterpointing myth, fiction and actuality through the device of a sort of writer's commonplace-book. There is no sense of recession, of one order of reality — myth or novel or narration — lying behind another: all are on the same level of importance, and this is what gives the contrapuntal effect. The scope of fiction is both extended and limited — limited as to action (not much happens, though plenty is heard about) but extended as to technique. It is a very Irish book and very funny. But it still awaits the popularity it deserves.

The Power and the Glory

GRAHAM GREENE [1940]

In the USA this novel was entitled *Labyrinthine Ways*, which suggests pursuit by the Hound of Heaven. No title could be more inept. Greene's hero, the "whisky priest", is, despite all his massive human faults, the incarnation of God's power and glory, which are blotted out by the atheistic positivism of the Mexican dictatorship which puts priests high on the list of enemies of the state. Nowhere in his many novels has Greene better conveyed the torrid decay of tropical townships, where the carious ruins are metaphors for a world without God. His priest is pursued by the hounds of repression, but he clings fast to his vocation, administering the sacraments, giving sermons in jungle clearings and *pueblos*, looking for wine that he may say mass. The state is not merely atheistical, it is prohibitionist: the outlawing of wine, which can be turned into Christ's blood, is, in Greene's symbolism, the ultimate oppression. The most harrowing scene occurs when the priest has, by good luck, found a bottle of wine but has to suffer its being consumed in his presence by a corrupt state official. Though, at the end, he dies, another priest appears from nowhere: the ministry goes on, the power and the glory will not be denied. This book comes early in the list of those novels of Greene (most of them) which deal specifically with the place of the Catholic in a secular world and present priests who, carrying the referred glory and the actual power, can afford to be imperfect human beings. It seems to many now to be too Greenean to take seriously (early works often look, with the curse of hindsight, like self-parody), but it is distinguished and serious art even when we have ceased to be affected by its theology.

For Whom the Bell Tolls

ERNEST HEMINGWAY [1940]

This novel was a spectacular success even in Britain — where a bigger war than the Spanish struggle which the book is about was occupying people's minds. In the year of publication it sold 360,000 copies in the United States alone. Such success turned the literary critics against Hemingway: Edmund Wilson spoke of commercialization, concessions, selling out. The fact was that the "popular" novel of the American thirties had already absorbed so many Hemingwayesque elements that what had once been experimental was now part of every second-rate novelist's technical inventory. Hemingway here had not overtaken himself, nor his imitators: the earlier novels still strike the reader with a sense of freshness and original power; *For Whom the Bell Tolls* has merely the expected stylistic felicities. For any other writer it would have been a great masterpiece. As it is, it is the best fictional report on the Spanish Civil War that we possess.

The strength lies in the literary style — clean, simple, with dialogue that catches the Spanish idiom. Certain scenes and symbols have a classic ring — Maria and Robert Jordan's night of love, when the earth can be felt moving beneath their "alliance against death"; the "solid flung metal grace" of the bridge, which is the one link between the opposed forces and also, in a wider view, the way by which the new age of mechanical regimentation will overtake the old pastoral world of simple needs and loyalties. Robert Jordan, the American professor of Spanish who fights for the Loyalists, an intellectual who seems ignorant of Marxist ideology, only just convinces; Maria, raped and shorn by the fascists, is not quite as compelling as Tolstoy's Natasha, despite Hemingway's ambition and boast, but she and the formidable Pilar are the best-made of all Hemingway's female characters. The dignity of the author's aim — to speak the truth about love and pain and courage in the traditional high romantic manner — has to be applauded. Hemingway avoids the temptation to turn his book into Loyalist propaganda: the left wing is no exemplification of incorrupt and shining chivalry. Like all art, the book is complex, even ambivalent. It taught millions to love or hate Spain, but it could not leave them indifferent.

Strangers and Brothers

C.P. SNOW [1940-70]

This sequence of eleven large novels is, unlike Anthony Powell's comparable *roman fleuve*, concerned with time as a treadmill, not as a Proustian plasticity which can turn into music and accompany a dance. The constituent books trace the course of modern history straightforwardly, as follows: *Strangers and Brothers* — 1925-33; *The Conscience of the Rich* — 1927-36; *Time of Hope* — 1914-33; *The Light and the Dark* — 1935-43; *The Masters* — 1937; *Homecomings* — 1938-48; *The New Men* — 1939-46; *The Affair* — 1953-54; *Corridors of Power* — 1955; *The Sleep of Reason* — the 1960s, particularly the time of the Moors Murders; *Last Things* — the end of the decade. We may sometimes go back in time, but we always move forward to the emergence of some large truth about the nature of our era.

The sequence takes the form of the autobiography of Lewis Eliot — later Sir Lewis Eliot, though, unlike his creator, he never achieves a barony. He is the son of decent working-class people in the Midlands; his birthplace is probably Leicester, Snow's own town, and his birthtime is round about the First World War. He enters a divided world — the nature of which is indicated in the title *Strangers and Brothers*. Eliot has a deep, intuitive understanding of his brother and of two friends who stand in a kind of fraternal relationship to him; other people are strangers, external phenomena to be recorded and coolly analysed. The recording, commenting side of Eliot is not (as it is with Powell's Nicholas Jenkins) all we are allowed to see of him: he is an emotional man, though he keeps his emotions under control. He suffers in his first marriage: his upper-class wife is neurotic and likely to harm his legal career. His younger friend, the brilliant scholar Roy Calvert, is manic-depressive. Death ends both relationships: his wife commits suicide, Calvert is killed as a pilot on a bombing mission over Germany. About this latter, Snow writes with a bitterness echoed by many of us who lived through the war: the terribly erroneous strategic doctrine of the aerial offensive against "interior lines of communication" seemed to arise from some mysterious human darkness, against the light of reason.

Eliot flourishes as a barrister. As an external law lecturer at Cambridge he comes into contact with the world of academic politics, closely examined in *The Masters*. War breaks out, and he becomes a temporary civil servant. He meets the woman who is to become his second wife. She represents a new background; her father is a successful painter, contemptuous of or indifferent to the attitudes of society. One of the imponderables, for which the world of the Light cannot legislate, now attacks Eliot and his new wife: the illness of her first child suggests spiteful revenge on them for having defied the conventions and lived as lovers. But the mysterious power relents, leaving their relationship more firmly cemented than before.

Involved in the development of a nuclear deterrent, Eliot shares the horror of many of his scientific friends at its possibilities and sees his brother give up a promising career in scientific research because of his principles. Eliot now examines the "closed politics" of the decision-forming committees and enters the world admirably summed up in the title (now proverbial) *Corridors of Power*. The passage of Sir Lewis through the wonderland of high life reveals to him a division in society far greater than that of mere strangers and brothers: the rulers hardly know that the ruled exist. There had to be a descent on the part of the powerful into humanity. But humanity cannot always, so *The Sleep of Reason* tells us, be relied upon to be human. The central event of this novel is obviously derived from those Moors Murders of which Lady Snow (Pamela Hansford Johnson) wrote in *On Iniquity*.

This sequence is a very considerable achievement, despite the flatness of the writing and the almost wilful evasion of the mythic and poetic. It brings into the novel themes and locales never seen before (except perhaps in Trollope). Neglected since Snow's death, it deserves to be reconsidered as a highly serious attempt to depict the British class system and the distribution of power. The work has authority: it is not the dream of a slippered recluse but of a man actively involved in the practical mechanics of high policy-making.

The Aerodrome

REX WARNER [1941]

This is a novel which many of us sought during the war (in which books were published, snapped up and then disappeared) but for the most part only read or heard about. We knew, having read the same author's *The Wild Goose Chase*, published in 1937, that it would probably be very British but also very much under the influence of Franz Kafka. Warner had taken from Kafka the device of the mysterious allegory and the atmosphere of threat and guilt. Going home from Gibraltar by troopship in 1945 I found three copies in the ship's library and at once devoured one of them. The story concerns a small village — undoubtedly in England, though there is no specification of place (just like Kafka). The village represents the fallen human condition — unregenerate but moderately happy. The villagers get drunk in the pub; a man bites the heads off live rats for pints of beer; there is copulation in the hedgerows and a certain amount of suspected incest about. On the outskirts of the village a huge aerodrome is built, and the airforce (not the RAF we know) takes over the area in the name of the state. The state, of which the air force is the dynamic agent, prepares to do battle with sinful human nature. Original sin is to be cast out, there is to be no more muddle and irrationality; the future is to be clean, healthy, disciplined, totalitarian. Above all, the family, the product of filthy sex as well as the source of morbid fixations, is to be abolished. Ironically, it is because of the unsuspected family links between the air vice-marshal — a great figure of authority and the voice of the new morality — and some members of the village community that the monstrous takeover fails. The tyrannical lord of the aerodrome is killed by a bomb planted by his own son at the time of the launching of the first pilotless aircraft. The scheme whereby the whole of the country (unnamed, but it seems to be England) is to be purified and disciplined comes to nothing. Unregenerate life returns, complete with drunkenness and hedgerow fornication. It has, paradoxically, its own purity, while the aspiration of total order is filthy: " 'That the world may be clean': I remember my father's words. Clean indeed it was and most intricate, fiercer than tigers, wonderful and infinitely forgiving."

The Horse's Mouth

JOYCE CARY [1944]

Cary always wrote his novels in groups. The trio consisting of *Herself Surprised, To Be a Pilgrim* and *The Horse's Mouth* concerns itself with three characters, each of whom takes the foreground in turn. Sara Munday in the first tells of her love-life with Wilcher (who takes the lead in the second) and with Gulley Jimson, who dominates the third. It is best to regard this trinity as a unity, but *The Horse's Mouth* stands up well on its own (it was, incidentally, superbly filmed with Alec Guinness in the lead).

Gulley Jimson is a painter of genius, and Cary, who once studied the art, understands him very well. Jimson is a total nonconformist and his god is William Blake, whom he quotes endlessly in his somewhat Joycean interior monologues. Like Blake, he believes that imagination represents a higher order of reality than what dull people call the real world. Only his art has meaning for him, though it has little meaning in the postwar age which tolerates him as a harmless anachronism. Old and impoverished, in and out of jail, Jimson unscrupulously gets money, paint and canvas where he can: art is his only morality. To emphasize his indifference to the world, he brings his story to its glorious catastrophic end by painting a huge mural depicting the Creation of the World on the wall of a building that is already being demolished. The book is crammed with characters and picaresque episodes, and its fire and gusto never once flag. It is a comic hymn to life, but it has nobility as well. Depicting low life, it blazes with an image of the highest life of all — that of the creative imagination. Sara Munday is an admirable complement to Jimson. From the angle of orthodoxy — and religiously she is very orthodox — Sara is a great sinner, but she is one of those sinners who proclaim the wonder of the life of the flesh, like Juliet's nurse or the Wife of Bath. "Everything that lives is holy," said Blake, and both Sara and Jimson are holy in their whole-hearted capacity to give of themselves, reserving moral doubts till later — very much later. Cary was a great novelist.

The Razor's Edge

WILLIAM SOMERSET MAUGHAM [1944]

Somerset Maugham's most massive novel was *Of Human Bondage* (1915), his most satisfying *Cakes and Ale* (1930). He published *The Razor's Edge* at the age of seventy, and one is entitled to marvel at his grasp of the problems of a generation far junior to his, as well as a total lack of fatigue in the handling of a complex narrative structure. He evades problems of literary style, and he always did, by placing himself firmly in the scene — sceptical, reasonable, urbane — as a spectator and recorder, telling his story with the dry directness of a skilled club or dinner party raconteur. His main character, Larry, is very nearly the sole example in all his work of a personage wholly good — even wholly holy. The title refers to the mode of life which Larry learns to adopt after his earnest, but not pompous, search for a *tao* or way. Materially, one must live on the razor edge between poverty and minimal subsistence in order to cultivate the life of the spirit. Maugham was ahead of his time in pointing to Indian Vedanta as a system which was likely to appeal to a generation sickened by the failure of the West to promote the good life. Reading, one suspects that the various strands of the narrative are woven with too great casualness, but one realizes at the end that there was, after all, a unity, apart from the factitious one of friendship and family — all the characters, even Sophie, who succumbs to drink, dissolution and a violent death, get what they want: the principle of free will applies to all and is fundamentally the one thing that counts. A master of the short story form, Maugham frequently had difficulty with the bigger structures, but this sizeable novel is a formal triumph as well as a moving and enlightening study of human desires, agonies, triumphs.

Brideshead Revisited

EVELYN WAUGH [1945]

The creation of a television series based on this book (in 1981) was a pretext for reappraisal of the book itself. The general consensus was that *Brideshead Revisited* was a sham and a snobbish sham. This referred as much to Waugh's recension of the book in 1960 (he trimmed off the fat, meaning the gluttony appropriate to deprived wartime but reprehensible in peace) as to the self-indulgent first version. Everything in the novel would seem to be wrong — the implausible invention of a rich English aristocratic family haunted by the God of the Catholics; the Hound of Heaven pursuing the agnostic narrator-hero; the implication that only the upper class may be taken seriously. Charles Ryder, who tells the story, is seduced by Brideshead Castle and its denizens: but this seduction is merely the prelude to his improbable seduction by God. The eschatological does not sit well with the sybaritic. And so on. And so on.

And yet. And yet. I have read *Brideshead Revisited* at least a dozen times and have never failed to be charmed and moved, even to tears. It is, appropriately, a seductive book. Even the overblown metaphors move and charm. The comedy is superb: Mr Samgrass, Ryder's father, Anthony Blanche are wonderful portraits. And the evocation of pre-war Oxford and Venice, where Ryder "drowns in honey", is of great brilliance. This is one of those disturbing novels in which the faults do not matter. (Increasingly one finds that the greatest works of literary art are those with the most flaws — *Hamlet*, for instance.) Waugh's regular Augustan stance, suitable for a comic writer, becomes confused with one romantic as a blown rose by moonlight, but it does not matter. Apart from its literary qualities, it breathes a theological certainty which, if a little too *chic*, is a world away from the confusions of Greeneland and the squalor of the Irish It is a novel altogether readable and damnably magical.

Titus Groan

MERVYN PEAKE [1946]

This is the first book of a trilogy which continues with *Gormenghast* (1950) and concludes with *Titus Alone* (1959), but it may well be read — and perhaps ought to be read — as a self-contained work or solitary masterpiece. It is a mad book full of "Gothic" writing like this: "This tower, patched unevenly with black ivy, arose like a mutilated finger from among the fists of knuckled masonry and pointed blasphemously at heaven." The knuckled masonry belongs to the great castle of Gormenghast, of which Titus becomes the seventy-seventh earl, proclaimed as such by the Warden of the Immemorial Rites. At the end of the book Titus is not quite two years old, but there are so many other weird personages bustling about in this dark closed world that we can afford to defer our meeting him until the next book — if, that is, we feel inclined to. Gormenghast is sustained by tradition and ritual. Lord Sepulchrave, Titus's father, is instructed daily by Sourdust, lord of the library, in symbolic gestures, strange dresses, a complicated liturgy. Only by ritual can life be sustained. Even in the Great Kitchen there are eighteen faceless men called the Grey Scrubbers, whose lowly work is predestined and hereditary, as though it were sacerdotal. Everybody in the castle has a fixed and immutable office — Rottcodd (curator of the Hall of the Bright Carvings), Flay, Swelter, Steerpike, Mrs Slagg, Prunesquallor — a gallery of glorious and very British eccentrics. Only young Steerpike, who emerges from the lowliness of the kitchens, defies the immemorial order and preaches a sort of revolution. He calls the Countess of Groan, that great lady who lives in a sea of white cats, "the old Bunch of Rags". Pulling the legs off a stagbeetle, he prates about equality. Eventually he breaks into an orgy of destruction, burning the library, killing its lord, sending Titus's father mad. There is a season of violence and murder, but Gormenghast remains, indestructible. It is, if you wish, an allegory of what had been happening in Europe during the time when Peake was writing the book. But it is also pure fantasy, a totally original creation.

The Victim

SAUL BELLOW [1947]

This, Bellow's second novel, is the only one that deals specifically with antisemitism. This theme was popular in the immediately postwar American novel, but it was often treated in a superficial manner — as in Arthur Miller's *Focus*, where a man is persecuted because he *looks* like a Jew (whatever a Jew looks like) and the basic reasons for antisemitism are not considered. In *The Victim*, Bellow shows that the Jew and the Jew-baiter are, in a sense, necessary to each other. Albee, the antisemitic deadbeat, accuses the Jew Leventhal of getting on in the world at his, Albee's, expense. Leventhal sees that, although the particular accusation is groundless, there is truth in the general thesis that everyone gets on at the expense of others. Albee thus becomes a desirable focus of Leventhal's ordinary human guilt. And Albee's and Leventhal's sharpened awareness of the boundaries between themselves is a means of discovering and asserting identity. Albee becomes a kind of parasite on Leventhal, but the mutual enmity emerges as a genuine symbiosis. The parasite clings to the host, but clinging is an aspect of need, which is a way towards love.

Bellow's trademark is the popular-novel theme which is, through great richness of language and subtlety of insight, transformed into something highly distinguished. The bigger novels — *Herzog, Henderson the Rain King, Augie March* — are brilliant but a little shrill in comparison with this quiet early masterpiece.

Under the Volcano

MALCOLM LOWRY [1947]

This novel is a Faustian masterpiece which still awaits general recognition (the film may help). Like Joyce's *Ulysses*, it presents in detail the events of a single day in a single place — the Day of the Dead in a town in Mexico, with Popocatepetl and Ixtaccihuatl looking down. It is the last day on earth of the British Consul, Geoffrey Firmin, and he is dying of alcoholism. Like any tragic hero, he is fully aware of the choice he has made: he clings to his sloth, he needs salvation through love but will not utter the word which will bring it, he lets his morbid lust for drink drag him from bar to bar. In other words, he has made a deliberate choice of damnation. He is already, in a sense, in hell, for Mexico is diabolic and the world outside is ready to plunge itself into the Second World War. At the end of the book he is somewhat casually murdered, and his body is thrown into the ravine between the volcanoes, with a dead dog after it.

We don't despise or even dislike Firmin, despite his weaknesses and his self-destructive urge. As with all tragic heroes (and this novel is a genuine tragedy) he sums up the flaws which are latent or actual in all of us: like Marlowe's Faustus, he excites pity and terror. He has tasted of the world as it is — corrupt, violent — and he sees contemporary history as symptomatic of the rottenness which is built into the human condition. He sees this with a preternatural clarity (that gift the gods grant to all tragic heroes) and he exercises the free will which enables him to opt out of the personal and public mess. But he recognizes that free will is never total: he did not make the world. He is a martyr or witness and also a victim.

The plot is not everything here. Lowry's use of flashback, interior monologue and symbol is highly idiosyncratic, but the work belongs to the tradition which began with *Ulysses*. *Ulysses* was supposed to be, by 1947, well digested by the intelligent reading public and the publishers who serve it, but one has only to read Lowry's correspondence with his publisher to see how imperfectly his artistic aims were understood. By the end of the century *Under the Volcano* may be seen as one of its few authentic masterpieces.

The Heart of the Matter

GRAHAM GREENE [1948]

Evelyn Waugh's Guy Crouchback, in the war trilogy *Sword of Honour* (q.v.), pays a great compliment to this novel of Greene's. He is in West Africa in 1941. In 1948 he reads *The Heart of the Matter* and is asked "Was West Africa like that?" He replies: "It *must* have been like that." The evocation of time and place — the laterite roads, the flapping of the vultures on the metal roofs, the sweat and the rain — is done with exact economy.

Waugh himself was unsure, however, about the theology of the book. It is about a colonial police officer named Scobie, a Catholic convert married to a cradle Catholic named Louise ("literary Louise" is what the philistines of the club call her). Louise, sick of West Africa, takes a holiday in South Africa, with money which Scobie has borrowed from an untrustworthy Syrian trader. While she is away Scobie is deputed by his chief to take care of some shipwrecked civilians, victims of a German torpedo. He falls in love with a young widow. though the motives of the unwise affair that ensues are grounded more in pity than in passion. As always happens in a British colony, the affair, despite the careful secrecy with which it is conducted, becomes common knowledge. Louise in South Africa hears about it and comes home, though she does not disclose her knowledge. She thinks to put an end to the affair by asking Scobie to go to communion with her at Christmas. He will have to confess adultery before taking the eucharist and will, presumably, vow not to continue in the sin. But Scobie cannot condemn his young mistress to misery and loneliness. He does not repent and he makes a sacrilegious communion.

Loving two women at the same time had damned him. He determines to cast himself out thoroughly from God by compounding sacrilege with suicide. Louise is convinced of his damnation, but the local priest, Father Rank, is not so sure. The Church, he says, knows little of the human soul: men don't go to a priest to confess their virtues. Thus the book ends on a heretical note. We cannot believe that Scobie is in hell. It is even implied, by a careful deployment of symbols, that Scobie is really a saint. Evelyn Waugh was unhappy about this and condemned the book's message from an intransigently orthodox angle, along with the Vatican itself (though Pope Paul confessed to Greene that he had read it). Aesthetically, however, Waugh considered the work to be masterly.

It is, in fact, a work of brilliant economy, very moving — even to non-Catholics (though my Muslim students to whom I taught the book in Malaysia thought Scobie's situation ridiculous). Casting doubt on ecclesiastical doctrine that is specifically Catholic, the novel may be considered more sectarian than universal, but it is concerned with real human dilemmas and its presentation of scene and atmosphere is altogether brilliant.

Ape and Essence

ALDOUS HUXLEY [1948]

This brief novel was written under the shadow of Hiroshima. After the dropping of the atom bomb many writers were obsessed with the prospect of a Third World War which could not be long delayed and which would, through the employment of nuclear weapons, wipe out civilization. We have been waiting forty years for that war and it has not yet transpired; we have stopped writing novels about it. Novels like *Ape and Essence* seem now to be very much products of their time and rather dated. But this is Huxley — clever, brutal, thoughtful, original — and his fictional tract clings to the mind.

The novel is presented in the form of a rejected film script. This shape enables the author to indulge in visual fantasy, whereby men are turned into apes and voices singing words of Goethe ("*Das Ewgi-Weibliche zieht uns hinan*") accompany a shot of spermatozoa wriggling into the ova. A female ape sings:

> Love love love love's the very essence
> Of everything I say, everything I do.
> Give me give me give me give me detumescence —
> That means you.

There are no illusions about man and his high ideals. Nuclear man has reverted to the simian.

Woven into the fantasy is a story set in Southern California after the World War which puts an end to civilisation. Worship in Belial has replaced Christianity. After all, the atom bomb is diabolic, and the devil may drop it again unless he is placated with prayer and human sacrifice. Sex is banned, except for seasonal orgies which produce hideous mutations that can be mactated in Belial's name. The heroine, who falls in love with a visiting New Zealand scientist, is considered physically normal, since she merely has supernumerary nipples. It is a nauseating vision of a still possible future and, as this is Huxley, a very full intellectual summation of man's self-damnation is put into the mouth of one of the characters — a castrated elder of the Californian tribe. All of human history has deferred to the diabolic: as a man sows, so shall he reap.

The Naked and the Dead

NORMAN MAILER [1948]

The British edition of this novel appeared in 1949, the same year as *Nineteen Eighty-Four*, and percipient critics saw that the two books had in common the theme of a new doctrine of power. Winston Smith's torturer in *Nineteen Eighty-Four* (q.v.) presents his victim-pupil with an image of the future — a boot stamping on a face for ever and ever. General Cummings in Mailer's novel tells Lieutenant Hearn to see the Army as "a preview of the future", and it is a future very like Orwell's, its only morality "a power morality". He, representing the higher command, and Sergeant Croft, the lower, are fighting fascism but are themselves fascists and well aware of it. Hearn, the weak liberal who will not, despite his weakness, submit to the sadism of Cummings, is destroyed by his general through his sergeant. Cummings the strategist plans while Croft the fighting leader executes; Hearn, who represents a doomed order of human decency, is crushed between the two extremes of the new power morality.

The narrative presents, with great accuracy and power, the agony of American troops in the Pacific campaign. A representative group of lower-class Americans forms the reconnaissance patrol sent before a proposed attack on the Japanese-held island of Anopopei. We smell the hot dishrag effluvia of the jungle and the sweat of the men. Of this body of typical Americans, however, despite the vivid realization of skin, muscle and nerves, only Hearn and Croft emerge as living individuals. With the men there is an over-zealous desire to range the racial and regional gamut of the United States — the Jew, the Pole, the Texan and so on. Mailer blocks in their backgrounds with a device borrowed from John Dos Passos — the episodic fragmentary impressionistic flashback, which he calls "The Time Machine". This is something of a mill or grinder: it seems to reduce the pasts of all the subsidiary characters to the common flour of sexual preoccupation.

The futility of war is well presented. The island to be captured has no strategic importance. The spirit of revolt among the men is stirred by an accident: the patrol stumbles into a hornets' nest and runs away, dropping weapons and equipment, the naked leaving the dead behind them. An impulse can contain the seeds of human choice: we have not yet been turned entirely into machines. Mailer's pessimism was to come later — in *The Deer Park* and *Barbary Shore* and *An American Dream* — but here, with men granting themselves the power to opt out of the collective suicide of war, there is a heartening vision of hope. This is an astonishingly mature book for a twenty-five-year-old novelist. It remains Mailer's best, and certainly the best war novel to emerge from the United States.

No Highway

NEVIL SHUTE [1948]

Nevil Shute disclaimed any high literary intention in the writing of his novels. He was a no-nonsense engineer who worked on the airship R-101 and whose autobiography is entitled *Slide Rule*. But he had imagination, and some of his themes are enhanced by the plain style in which he wrote. Thus, *In the Wet* looks first at an England grown grey and spiritless with socialism and the over-levelling of a one-man one-vote universal franchise, finally transferring the British monarchy — beset by the snarling republicans of the Left — to Australia. In *On the Beach* we have another Australian narrative: the antipodes awaits the drift, from the already extinguished northern hemisphere, of the radiation sickness which is the legacy of World War III. The people of Melbourne await the end with commendable phlegm, having closed their minds to the impending disaster. This comes, however, and only Shute is there to describe it. This is the only true "close-ended" novel ever written. No character exists after the final page, but it would be cruel to suggest that no character exists before it either. The creation of living Tolstoyan personages was not Shute's strong suit. After all, he was an engineer.

But *No Highway* does contain credible characters, not least the hero, a boffin who tries to persuade his unconvinced colleagues of the reality of metal fatigue in aircraft. The concept was not taken seriously at the time when the book was written, and *No Highway* must be looked on with awe as a rare novel that has changed not social thinking but aerodynamic doctrine. The courage of a dim disregarded theoretical engineer in sticking to convictions that are derided, his domestic life with his motherless daughter (who has the gift of extrasensory perception) and his bizarre relationship with a famous film star (one of the passengers on the fatigued plane he ruthlessly grounds) are presented with sharp humour and compassion. It is also good to have a novel so firmly based on the facts of the world of technology.

The Heat of the Day

ELIZABETH BOWEN [1948]

No novel has better caught the atmosphere of London during the Second World War. Elizabeth Bowen conveys that drab suffering world in such intense and credible detail that it conjures sensuous and emotional memories (in any reader who knew that time and place) so heightened that one seems to be re-living them. But the novel is much more than this and it is even much more than the story of Stella Rodney, who falls in love with Robert Kelway, a man discharged from the services after Dunkirk who, wounded in body and in mind, becomes a traitor. The war crystallizes for the author the problem of where to look for assurance when a civilization breaks down. "The private cruelty and the world war both have their start in the heated brain." Stella's wartime situation — living in a rented flat where nothing is hers and where her love affair is carried on with no sense of permanence and continuity — is symbolic of the death of tradition. When Stella visits the home of Robert's family, Holme Dene, she asks: "How can anyone live in a place that has for years been asking to be brought to an end?" The house is no emblem of permanency, merely a place bought to sell at a profit. The roots of Robert's treachery lie in such artificiality and impermanence. Meanwhile in neutral Ireland images of reality are to be found — the "big houses" set in landscapes which mock human pretensions and teach man his place in nature. Holme Dean in England is set against Mount Morris in Ireland. The former, with its "swastika-arms of passages leading to nothing", grants nothing except an artificial moral sense which has replaced human compassion. Robert becomes a victim of an abstraction — the belief that Nazi Germany represents a new order to which he can attach himself. Mount Morris, on the other hand, embodies the marriage of past and present; a tradition which transcends the self and curbs the ego, "the heated brain." This outline sounds simplistic, but the novel, with its economy and sharp elegant writing, suggests answers to the human predicament, expressed in exactly chosen symbols.

Nineteen Eighty-Four

GEORGE ORWELL [1949]

This is one of the few dystopian or cacotopian visions which have changed our habits of thought. It is possible to say that the ghastly future Orwell foretold has not come about simply because he foretold it: we were warned in time. On the other hand, it is possible to think of this novel as less a prophecy than the comic joining together of two disparate things — an image of England as it was in the immediate post-war era, a land of gloom and shortages, and the bizarrely impossible notion of British intellectuals taking over the government of the country (and, for that matter, the whole of the English-speaking world). The world is divided into three superstates — Oceania, Eurasia and Eastasia, two of which, in a perpetual shifting of alliances, are always at war with the other. Britain is part of Oceania and is called Airstrip One. Winston Smith, a citizen of its capital, has been brought up, like everyone else, to accept the monolithic rule of Big Brother — a mythical and hence immortal being, the titular head of an oligarchy which subscribes to a philosophy called, ironically, English Socialism or Ingsoc. Only the "proles", the masses, are free, free because their minds are too contemptible to be controlled; members of the Party are under perpetual surveillance from the Thought Police. Winston, the last man to possess any concept of freedom (the title Orwell originally envisaged for the book was *The Last Man in Europe*), revolts against Big Brother, but he is arrested and — through torture allied to metaphysical re-education — rehabilitated. He learns the extent of the power of the Party, its limitless ability to control thought, even speech. Newspeak is a variety of English which renders it impossible to express an heretical thought; "doublethink" is a technique which enables the Party to impress its own image on external reality, so that "2+2 = 5" can be a valid equation. The State is eternal and absolute, the only repository of truth. The last free man yields, of his own free will (this is important — there is no brainwashing in Orwell's cacotopia), his whole being to it.

Aldous Huxley admitted, in re-introducing his *Brave New World* (1932 — outside our scope) to the post-war age, that Orwell presented a more plausible picture of the future than he himself had done, with his image of a world made stable and happy through chemical conditioning. Whether Orwell himself, were he alive today, would withdraw any part of his prophecy (if it *is* a prophecy) we do not know. He was mortally sick when he made it, admitting that it was a dying man's fantasy. The memorable residue of *Nineteen Eighty-Four*, as of *Brave New World*, is the fact of the tenuousness of human freedom, the vulnerability of the human will, and the genuine power of applied science.

Nineteen Eighty-Four is not a perfect novel, and some would argue that it is too didactic to be considered a novel at all. Orwell's best work is to be found in the four posthumously published volumes of critical and polemical essays, and in his fable *Animal Farm* (1945). This last is certainly not a novel and hence cannot be considered for inclusion here.

The Body

WILLIAM SANSOM [1949]

This novel deals with a very old theme — marital jealousy. A middle-aged hairdresser comes to believe that his wife, equally mature though still ripely attractive, is having an affair with a hearty, convivial, practical-joke-loving neighbour. His jealousy, like Othello's, has no foundation, but, unlike Othello, he is driven not to uxoricidal madness but to an obsession with seeing his cuckoldry confirmed. He watches closely and his eyes are sharpened; the details of the external world come through with a clarity which is abnormal but not, I think, hallucinatory. Sansom's ear, matching his eye, renders the idioms and rhythms of post-war lower-middle-class English with a frightening exactness. The final image that emerges in the self-tortured brain of the husband is of the human body growing old and unsavoury — the broken toenails, the rough skin, the bad breath — and the sexual urge as a kind of insentient insanity. It is what the sharpened eye is led to observe at last and it leads, in its turn, to a kind of resigned philosophy. By a paradox, Sansom mines into the human spirit by staying on the surface.

The banality of the plot is typical of Sansom. What is important to him is the manipulation of words to serve a highly pictorial end. This novel, like Sansom's better-known short stories, educates the reader into taking a fresh, as it were rain-washed, look at the world of visual sensation. But there is emotional power here and a very acute intelligence.

Scenes from Provincial Life

WILLIAM COOPER [1950]

In America this book has been amalgamated with *Scenes from Married Life* (1961) to form a single novel called *Scenes from Life.* The sequel is inferior to the original. In the first book we have the first of the British anti-heroes, Joe Lunn, a science master in a grammar school who refuses to conform, either in taste or behaviour, with dull provincial society, though his rejection of the bourgeois way of life never touches criminality. The trouble with him is that he believes in nothing strongly enough to wish to oppose it to the gods of the borough; he is an anarchist who would be less at home in an anarchical society than he is in a bourgeois one. From the sequel we learn what we all along expected to learn — that Joe had become a respectable civil servant and a reputable novelist, and all that he now needs to brim his cosy content is the status of husband and father. Stendhal's Julien Sorel in *Le Rouge et le Noir* — the distant progenitor of all anti-heroes — goes the whole hog in his disruption of bourgeois society; the British rebels, starting with Joe Lunn, merely have a fling before settling down.

Scenes from Provincial Life must be taken as an entertaining portrait of a small good-hearted rebel, too feeble to make his protest against society seem more than a clown's gesture, not even articulate enough to clarify for himself what precisely is wrong with society, except that it is full of humbug. Lower-middle or working-class Voltaires crying *"Ecrasez l'infâme!"* have grown out of societies quite unlike pre-revolutionary France; they are children of communities with enough food and no poverty, fractious sons of the Welfare State. As the prototype of a whole movement in British fiction, Cooper's novel has its importance. In its own right it has immense entertainment value and deserves to survive.

The Disenchanted

BUDD SCHULBERG [1950]

Schulberg's father was one of the successful Hollywood producers of the nineteen-thirties, and the son is perhaps best known as the scenarist of *On the Waterfront, A Face in the Crowd* and *The Harder They Fall*, though these last two are adaptations of Schulberg's own distinguished fiction. No film has yet been made of *The Disenchanted*, perhaps because of its literary orientation (less cinematically appealing than union violence, pop messiahship and the corrupt world of boxing). The book is about Hollywood in the thirties, but it is also about a great decayed novelist, Manley Halliday, who is a thinly disguised Scott Fitzgerald. The young Schulberg was employed to assist the ailing and near-destitute Fitzgerald in the preparation of a script for a film entitled, in the novel, *Love on Ice*. A trip to a north-eastern university in winter, for the filming of ice carnival backgrounds, results here (fiction diverging from reality) in the great novelist's physical collapse, his being fired from the project, and his death from complications following untreated diabetes. The distinction of the novel lies in its very full portrait, complete with brilliantly authentic flashbacks to the years of glamour and success, of a writer who was once the voice of the irresponsible twenties and still lives in them. Shep, his assistant, is torn between admiration for Halliday's work and a committed radical political stance which contradicts everything Halliday stood for. The delineation of Jeri, Halliday's wife, is clearly an imaginative portrait of Zelda Fitzgerald, and the partygoing of the twenties, the life of the Côte d'Azur, the extravagant immorality of the great days of Hollywood are caught with a fidelity that is sometimes cunningly distorted into the hallucinatory. This is a haunting novel. No fiction has ever done better at presenting the inner torments of a writer in decline, nor at suggesting the fundamental nobility of artistic dedication.

A Dance to the Music of Time

ANTHONY POWELL [1951-75]

This is a *roman fleuve* or river-novel. Despite its immense length it has, like Proust's *A la recherche du temps perdu*, to be taken as a unity. It owes something to Proust and even begins with a Proustian event — past time conjured by a trivial incident. With Proust it is a madeleine dipped in tea. At the very beginning of *A Question of Upbringing* Nicholas Jenkins, the narrator of the entire sequence, sees workmen warming themselves at a brazier. "As the dark fumes floated above the houses, snow began to fall gently from a dull sky, each flake giving a small hiss as it reached the bucket...." The snow makes Jenkins think — "for some reason" — of the antique world — "legionaries in sheepskin warming themselves at a brazier...centaurs with torches cantering beside a frozen sea". The classical associations take him back to school, learning the classical languages. Then Widmerpool, one of the main characters of the sequence, appears as a schoolboy and the narrative proper begins.

A narrator-commentator is essential to the scheme, for the time presented is not clock-bound, it is one man's interpretation of temporal flow. Jenkins watches the characters move, but they do not march through time — their movements must be formalized into the patterns of a dance. Time can only provide the music if the narrator's hands can move freely up and down the temporal keyboard. But who and where are the dancers? Their stage is where the world of the artist overlaps with that of polite and fashionable society. Bohemians mingle with aristocrats and people of affairs. We are not allowed to see everything they do: Jenkins selects such gestures as will fit best into his choreography; and he is reticent about matters which readers of popular fiction expect a narrator to be only too eager to disclose — his own love-life, for instance.

The fastidiousness of selection is matched by the polished formality of the style — a style apt for high comedy and the leisurely unfolding of comic situations. But high comedy represents a limitation of fictional resource, and the vastness of the plan shows up the smallness of scope and a certain narrowness of temperament. In that opening to *A Question of Upbringing*, Jenkins thinks of "Poussin's scene in which the Seasons, hand in hand, facing outward, tread in rhythm to the notes of the lyre that the winged and naked greybeard plays." Then he imagines "Human beings, facing outward like the Seasons, moving hand in hand in intricate measure." It is not, on the face of it, a large enough concept for an epic scale.

Take *The Kindly Ones*, the sixth episode in the sequence. The kindly ones — the Eumenides, or Furies (termed kindly because we are scared of them) — preside over the two great wars of our century. These are brought together: the musical technique ignores chronology and makes of time an ornamental pond rather than a river. The first world war is heralded by a big comic build-up suitable for the second-act curtain of a nightmare farce — the maidservant Billson deranged by talk of a ghost and by Albert the cook's impending marriage and entering the dining-room stark naked ("I really thought familiarity was breeding contempt," says Jenkins's mother. "I certainly hoped so, with parlourmaids so terribly hard to come by.") The second war is fanfared with a charade of the Seven Deadly Sins; this is enacted in the mansion of Sir Magnus Donners. Everything seems to be frozen into tableaux.

Like Evelyn Waugh, Powell cannot take the lower classes seriously. But, though his characters are all drawn from the same register, he plays very formidable music. Widmerpool and Moreland and Sir Magnus and the many others — some of them farcical eccentrics in the Waugh manner — deserve places in the eternal fictional pantheon, and the ambitiousness of the project is matched by the urbane skill with which it is executed. This is a work we may not always like, but we cannot ignore it.

The Catcher in the Rye

J.D. SALINGER [1951]

This novel is a key-work of the nineteen-fifties in that the theme of youthful rebellion is first adumbrated in it, though the hero, Holden Caulfield, is more a gentle voice of protest, unprevailing in the noise, than a militant world-changer. Holden tells his story in a vernacular that has learned something from the Beats, very attractive, often funny, sometimes childishly pitiable. He is an adolescent who leaves his boarding-school to spend a weekend in New York, meeting taxi-drivers, a prostitute, his own young sister, finally a man whom he has always respected (one of the very few: nearly all adults are suspect) but who makes a homosexual pass at him. There is no real plot, only the acute observations of a boy alone in a world of hypocrisy and false values, a world which is a kind of comic hell because it needs love and does not know how to find it. What the inner voice of Holden is talking about is a need which comes before love — honesty — as well as the horror of the public American image which thinks it can get along without either. Love does not mean sex; Holden has a chill instinct towards celibacy: it is significant that the only people he meets who are truly good are two nuns. Love, however, does seem to have something to do with death (Holden idolizes a dead brother) and with the innocence that dies with pubescence. Holden has misheard the words of Burns's song about coming through the rye: he seems himself as a body who catches in the rye — catches the innocent playing in a ryefield who are in danger of falling over the unseen edge of a cliff. But the dream-task of saving the innocents before the world corrupts them is a hopeless one: Holden escapes from its hopelessness into mental illness, and he is writing his story while under psychiatric treatment.

The Catcher in the Rye was the culminating work of a series of stories, most of which carried the theme of a sick mind's redemption through the innocence of a child (as in *For Esmé with Love and Squalor*). Salinger's later works — *Franny, Zooey* and *Raise High the Roof Beam, Carpenters* — have disappointed his admirers, though they are the books they should have expected. It required boldness to present an attempt at solving the world's problems through a positive creed of love, though Salinger's crime is to close in, depicting a family of the elect (the Glass family), who are doing two things — ritually washing away the world's guilt; practising a synthetic religion that has elements of Christianity and Zen Buddhism in it. Holden at least confronts the dirty mass of sinning humanity, though it drives him to a mental home; the Glass family confronts only itself.

The Catcher in the Rye was a symptom of a need, after a ghastly war and during a ghastly pseudo-peace, for the young to raise a voice of protest against the failures of the adult world. The young used many voices — anger, contempt, self-pity — but the quietest, that of a decent perplexed American adolescent, proved the most telling.

A Chronicle of Ancient Sunlight

HENRY WILLIAMSON [1951-69]

The novels that make up this sequence are *The Dark Lantern, Donkey Boy, Young Philip Maddison, How Dear is Life, A Fox Under My Cloak, The Golden Virgin, Love and the Loveless, A Test to Destruction, The Innocent Moon, It Was the Nightingale, The Power of the Dead, The Phoenix Generation, A Solitary War, Lucifer Before Sunrise* and *The Gate of the World*. Few have read them all. In general, the sequence has failed to engage the critical and public attention it merits. This has something to do, undoubtedly, with Williamson's political stance, as expressed through his hero Philip Maddison. The earlier books are the best — Maddison growing up in the near-rural outskirts of London, the England of the period before the First World War most accurately and fragrantly caught. Maddison becomes a soldier and later an officer, and three volumes are devoted to one of the most encyclopaedic fictional accounts we have of what that war was like. In *It Was the Nightingale*, Maddison enters a world with which Williamson, on the strength of the remarkable *Tarka the Otter*, will always be associated. Much of the book is taken up with the search for a pet otter which, to Maddison, is a remnant of the life he spent with his wife, now dead in childbirth. This is at times almost unbearably poignant. In the later volumes a pro-Fascist tone prevails, highly disturbing, and an almost manic bitterness which is far from acceptable. Williamson's style is romantic, though rarely sentimental, and his sensuous response to nature is fresh and surprising. What the sequence lacks is a thematic unity which transcends a mere near-autobiographical record of life in this century. Compared with Anthony Powell and even C.P. Snow, Williamson has been untouched by the spirit of modernity. The work has to be recommended as a whole, but no reader who ignores the second half can be wholly blamed.

The Caine Mutiny

HERMAN WOUK [1951]

This Pulitzer-Prize-winning novel stands somewhere between Norman Mailer's *The Naked and the Dead* (q.v.) and James Jones's *From Here to Eternity*. It has some literary distinction — far more than Jones's book, much less than Mailer's — and its considerable length is appropriate to the weightiness of its subject. To the officers of the USS *Caine* their captain seems slowly revealed as not merely incompetent but mad: this needs the *longueurs* of many voyages and the accumulation of many incidents to manifest itself beyond question. An intellectual officer (who is writing a long novel not unlike Wouk's own) nags on about the necessity of deposing the captain, but to him it is a mere game — disaffection without action. The first officer, however, takes him seriously and assumes control of the ship during a storm which shows up the captain's incompetence and hysteria. The mutineers are acquitted at the court martial which follows, thanks to a tricky legal officer adept at forensic cunning, but there is no real triumph. The gulf between the American intellectual, fundamentally irresponsible, and the professional serviceman who protects his way of life is presented with bitter honesty.

Herman Wouk is rarely accepted by "intellectual" literary critics as a novelist of power and achievement. He seems to lack depth in the delineation of character and distinction of style. But there are compensatory qualities which, to me, render the two massive later books — *The Winds of War* and *War and Remembrance* — valuable and highly impressive. No writer has worked harder at the amassing of the historical facts about World War II. For that matter, no writer has ever written with such authority about the trials of the life of the writer himself: *Youngblood Hawke*, stylistically undistinguished as it is, is the only novel we have which brutally gives the facts about profit and loss accounts, the hard graft of writing, the Balzacian details of the sordour and the literary life. But *The Caine Mutiny* remains Wouk's best book and it is likely to survive.

Invisible Man

RALPH ELLISON [1952]

This is without doubt the most important post-war novel on the condition of the black man in an intolerant white society. The black narrator calls himself invisible because "people refuse to see me.... When they approach me they see only my surroundings, themselves, or figments of their imagination — indeed, everything and anything except me." The reality of the narrator, who stands not only for all the blacks but for all the oppressed, is ignored; he appears to the outside world as a mere *thing* — to be tolerated, patronized, jeered at or kicked. The technique, which has elements of dream in it, like Kafka, and makes large use of symbolism, is a fluid picaresque one. Parts of the book can be taken as allegorical, such as the episode in the paint factory whose slogan is "Keep America Pure with Liberty Paints". The job of the hero — nameless as well as invisible — is to make white paint by dropping some magical substance into black liquid. This, stirred by a black finger, is essential for the pure white: the black keeps America clean by becoming a scapegoat for its sins. There are apocalyptic visions of wholesale destruction, sacrifice, the end of the world; there is a dream of running that ends in castration; there is an escape to a symbolic black hole where the protagonist becomes truly invisible, though that cellar, containing something blacker and more vital than coal, is the eventual source of heat and light. The moral of the book is subtle, not at all the orthodox plea for integration or the impotent scream about Black Power: "Why, if they follow this conformity business they'll end up forcing me, an invisible man, to become white, which is not a colour but a lack of one." What we all need is the glory of diversity. When we can see the glory, there will be no need for talk of toleration. This is a very moving book.

The Old Man and the Sea

ERNEST HEMINGWAY [1952]

More of a novella than a novel (but where *does* one draw the line?) this warmed and encouraged millions and confirmed Hemingway's capture of the Novel Prize. The book is about courage maintained in the face of failure, a theme that could not fail to move and exalt. An old Cuban fisherman goes out with his boat and sights a great marlin. Like a matador with a bull, he feels drawn to the magnificent creature, so that, though one has to kill the other, he does not much mind who kills whom. In an almost religious humility, old Santiago says: "Never have I seen a greater, or more beautiful, or a calmer or more noble thing than you, brother. Come on and kill me." His willingness to die in an act of worship gains him a reward: he kills the fish, though he is at once tortured by remorse. "You killed him for pride and because you are a fisherman." As he hauls the huge fish home the sharks attack it: he is being punished for hubris. He reaches land trailing a big mutilated corpse. But Santiago has not, in his failure, really failed. He has shown a right pride and a right humility; he has dared and touched grandeur. "Man is not made for defeat. A man can be destroyed but not defeated." The simple tale is loaded, though not ostentatiously, with allegorical meanings which delighted the Sunday preachers. As an example of simple "declarative" prose it is unsurpassed in Hemingway's *œuvre.* Every word tells and there is not a word too many. Hemingway's long hours of learning the marlin-fisher's craft — hours which, according to his left-wing critics, he had wasted in an escapist reactionary pursuit — had paid off. Writers must know about things as well as words.

The Groves of Academe

MARY McCARTHY [1952]

Witty, learned, even ironically pedantic, this is one of the best of the American campus novels. The President of Jocelyn College in Pennsylvania sends a letter to Henry Mulcahy, a middle-aged instructor in literature, saying: "Your appointment will not be continued beyond the current academic year...." Mulcahy's response is violent: he is being fired because he was once a member of the Communist Party and, though now quiescent, still carries a membership card. His colleagues discuss his case at great length and, in the manner of pedants, often miss the point: Mulcahy deserves to be fired because of inefficiency, intransigence etc. A poetry conference is held at the college, and a poet, Keogh, attends it who claims an old friendship with Mulcahy — a friendship initiated at political meetings. Keogh is forced into making a statement to the President about Mulcahy's position vis à vis the Communist Party and denies that he was ever a member — merely a half-baked progressive who stood on the sidelines. Mulcahy hears of this and threatens exposure of academic witch-hunting. He cannot now be dismissed by the President, who himself is forced to resign; it is the only way in which Jocelyn College will ever be rid of Mulcahy, who, anyway, was being dismissed for reasons quite unrelated to political activities. This novel is very much a product of the Senator McCarthy period (no relation), but its portrait of a typical small American educational establishment is valid for all time. The characters approach caricature but are highly memorable. The intelligence of the author shines in every paragraph, and there are observations which lodge in the memory: beautiful people are monists, ugly ones are gnostics (the beautiful accept their reflection in the mirror; the ugly say the reality lies elsewhere); if you have the duty of washing the dishes, renounce the duty — this leaves you existentially free to wash the dishes. And so on.

Wise Blood

FLANNERY O'CONNOR [1952]

Flannery O'Connor had a short life — 1925-64 — but, in her fiction at least, lived it fiercely. A Roman Catholic from the American Bible Belt, she was preoccupied with sin, redemption, the figure of Christ, but this essentially religious novel presents the eternal verities grotesquely, comically, with a subtle dash of Kafka. Hazel Motes (a man, not a woman) comes back from the war to the city of Taulkinham, there to found a new, Christless, church. "I'm going to preach there was no Fall because there was nothing to fall from and no Redemption because there was no Fall and no Judgment because there wasn't the first two. Nothing matters but that Jesus was a liar." And again: "Where you came from is gone, where you thought you were going to never was there, and where you are is no good unless you can get away from it." She is looking at a perversion of Southern Protestantism from a Catholic angle, a grotesque situation in itself. Motes's resistance to the traditional ways of redemption is marked by a number of shockingly absurd incidents, all set in a deliberately narrow ambience — the rural South, the closed Southern mentality — but everything adds up to his inability to control his own fate: his death is a parody of Christ's.

Flannery O'Connor said: "The fiction writer presents mystery through manners, grace through nature, but when he finishes, there always has to be left over that sense of Mystery which cannot be accounted for by any human formula." Her work presents, very firmly and accurately, the physical world of the fundamentalist South, but the viewpoint is, as it were, eternal, and here comes the sense of Mystery. The renunciation of Christ is a way of affirming him. This novel is like no other — the individuality is intense, the comedy fierce, the truth undeniable.

Sword of Honour

EVELYN WAUGH [1952-61]

This work was not originally planned as a trilogy. *Men at Arms* came out in 1952, to be followed by *Officers and Gentlemen* in 1955. The author considered then that he had said all he had to say about the experiences of his near-autobiographical Guy Crouchback in the Second World War, but he changed his mind later and completed the sequence with *Unconditional Surrender* in 1961 (published in the United States as *The End of the Battle*). In 1966 he pruned and revised and issued the trilogy as a single novel in one volume. Most readers prefer to take the items severally and in their unrevised form (compare *Brideshead Revisited*).

Guy Crouchback is a Catholic gentleman with a *castello* in Italy and a private income. His wife has left him to indulge in a series of marital adventures and his religion forbids divorce and remarriage. He is lonely, dim, dull, and has rejected the current of life. The coming of war fires him with a crusading zeal, but he is in his late thirties and the fighting machine does not want him. Eventually he joins the Halberdiers, trains, sees action in Dakar, Crete, finally Jugo-Slavia. Waugh does not push Crouchback too much into the foreground at first. There is a fine galaxy of comic characters — the magnificent Apthorpe, Brigadier Ritchie-Hook, the uniformed clubmen, as well as some more lovable than the satirist Waugh was previously able to give us — honest professional soldiers like Colonel Tickeridge, old Mr Crouchback with his firm and simple faith, eventually Uncle Peregrine, a universally dreaded bore who is not boring. But the pathos of Crouchback's situation is woven strongly into the fine war reportage and the superb comic action. Virginia, his wife, divorced again, rejects his advances. His new bride, the army, is proving a slut. Disillusionment about the true purpose of the war grows with the entry of the Russians into the conflict.

The age of the gentleman is disappearing. Men whom Crouchback admires prove treacherous or cowardly. There is a new type of hero emerging, summed up in the failed officer and impostor Trimmer, a former ship's hairdresser. Trimmer sleeps with Virginia and begets a child on her. Crouchback and she re-consummate their marriage and ensure that a great Catholic family has an heir, though — by an irony appropriate to the new age — this child is really a proletarian by-blow. Crouchback survives the débâcle of Crete, is sickened by the "people's war" in the Balkans, feels the death-urge, regrets the passing of an old order of chivalry and humanity but, with the stoicism of his kind, makes unconditional surrender to history. He had much in common with the hero of Ford Madox Ford's *Parade's End* (a tetralogy of the First World War on which Waugh's work seems to be modelled) — Christopher Tietjens, the incorrupt and traduced gentleman of Christian ideals. What Ford's book did for one war, Waugh has done for the other. *Sword of Honour* is not merely the story of one man's battles; it is the whole history of the European struggle itself, told with verve, humour, pathos and sharp accuracy.

The Long Goodbye

RAYMOND CHANDLER [1953]

Chandler was once considered an admirable writer of low-class fiction, the story of crime and detection (despite the example of Wilkie Collins's *The Moonstone*) being regarded as ineligible for inclusion in the ranks of the serious novel. But Chandler is a serious writer, an original stylist, creator of a character, Philip Marlowe, as immortal as Sherlock Holmes, and of an ambience — Southern California — which colours one's attitude to the real location. This is perhaps the best of the Philip Marlowe series. Here Marlowe, the stoical and rather quixotic private eye, attempts to lose his old detachment from people and make friends with Terry Lennox, a weak but amiable man who is married to the daughter of a multimillionaire. The marriage is unsatisfactory; Lennox calls his wife, Sylvia, a tramp. The story becomes complicated when Sylvia is found bloodily murdered. Bribed heavily by his father-in-law, Lennox agrees to take the blame for the murder: he disappears into Mexico and is later reported dead. The case is officially closed and the great family name of Potter (that of the tycoon) cleared.

Marlowe now meets a popular novelist, Roger Wade, sick of his meretricious craft, a drunkard and former friend of Sylvia. Marlowe considers the possibility that Wade may have killed Sylvia when drunk and then blacked out the incident. Then Wade is found dead. Marlowe learns that his wife, Eileen, was once married to Lennox. She killed Sylvia out of jealousy and then killed Wade because of his unreliability: "He talked too much." At the end of the book Lennox reappears. Marlowe is disillusioned with him: his weakness of character has produced an unnecessary murder. Marlowe is hurt, but he soon reverts to his old cynicism. He needed friendship, but he is not going to get it. The world is a jungle; it is cynically given a veneer of order by the corrupt police. You can say goodbye to everybody, but never to them.

Romantic, tending towards a sentimentality it never quite reaches, *The Long Goodbye* is beautifully composed, with a taut economical style exactly suited to the narrator Marlowe. If this is not literature, what is?

Lucky Jim

KINGSLEY AMIS [1954]

Amis caught the mood of post-war restiveness in a book which, though socially significant, was, and still is, extremely funny. Jim Dixon, its anti-hero, is a lower-middle-class young man from the provinces who has no great pretensions to anything — charm, looks, learning, certainly not wealth. A stroke of luck has given him a job at a redbrick university as junior lecturer in History, but a rebellious streak, which often comes out as maladroitness, qualifies his desire to conform and keep his job. Unfortunately his professor is a monumental fool much given to cultural week-ends, complete with madrigal-singing and recorder-blowing, and Dixon has other crosses to bear in high places. He asks little from life — enough money for beer and cigarettes, a nice undemanding girl friend — but society has so organized matters that he cannot have even this little. What he can have, what in fact is imposed upon him, is the great post-war sense of social purpose, hypocritical shibboleths about education, culture, progress. He asks for the bread of minimal comfort (along with the rest of a Britain that was sick of war and post-war austerity), but he is handed the stone of a spurious idealism.

Dixon is a radical, but radicalism is in his blood rather than in his head. He tests privilege and phony upper-class values, and he finds these extravagantly personified in Bertrand Welch, the son of his professor. To make things worse, Bertrand has a girl friend whom Dixon hopelessly desires. One of the big themes of *Lucky Jim* — and it is a theme to be found in much fiction and drama of the nineteen-fifties (John Osborne's *Look Back in Anger*, for instance) — is that of hypergamy — bedding a woman of a social class superior to one's own: this is an aspect of the perennial class motif of British fiction. Dixon achieves this aim, and others as well. He perpetrates enormities terrible enough to ensure his losing tenure (setting fire to Mrs Welch's bedclothes, collapsing drunk after a rebellious manifesto at a public lecture) and he gets something better — the job that Bertrand was after, Bertrand's girl friend. He makes little dents in the smug fabric of hypocritical, humbugging, class-bound British society, but he is not big enough to portend its collapse. His is the voice of decent protest, and it is a voice that a smug stable society finds it convenient to ignore.

Although we are intended to be on Jim Dixon's side, we are also intended to laugh at him, to pity his ignorance and ineptitude. There is a certain ambivalence in *Lucky Jim*, which shows itself also in Amis's other novels. The author, like his anti-heroes, is against culture because culture has the wrong associations — with Professor Welch and the rest of the phonies. At the same time he cannot hide the fact of his bookishness and musicality, and the Amis protagonist usually earns his living by purveying culture (as teacher, librarian, journalist or publisher). In *I Like It Here* Bowen has to apologise to himself for mentioning Elgar or Byron. The librarian hero of *That Uncertain Feeling* lives among books but reads only science fiction and cheesecake magazines. And yet the love-hate attitude to culture (it is not a matter of pure indifference) permeates the very prose-rhythms. All of Amis's novels, despite their high spirits, show up the sickness of a divided society. *Lucky Jim* is more than just a good laugh.

Room at the Top

JOHN BRAINE [1957]

One is reluctant to give this a place among what seem to be the most enduring works of fiction in the last forty-odd years, chiefly because the author himself makes such extravagant claims for it, but *Room at the Top* has considerable historical interest and is well if conventionally composed. It is a study in provincial hypergamy (or bedding a woman from a class superior to one's own) but very different from *Lucky Jim* — chiefly in its lack of humour and irony. Braine's working-class hero, Joe Lampton, is more ambitious than Amis's Jim Dixon. Coming to work in a large provincial Yorkshire town from a slummy outpost of depression, he demands more than a sufficiency of material comforts and a chance to sneer at the pretensions of the middle class. He wants the best and gets it through the door of seduction of, and inevitable marriage to, a magnate's daughter. His triumph over his upbringing and his natural instincts is, however, a qualified one: the woman he really loves (a married woman who represents no exalted future for him) dies a horrible death when he abandons her. If we want to see the nature of Joe's triumph, we have to read the disappointing sequel *Life at the Top*. The top seems not so very high — a large suburban house, children, a company car, a cocktail cabinet, business lunches in London, mutual adultery. But the implied moral of *Room at the Top* is spelt out: stay true to your class. British society is not really so mobile as it appears: the way up is available only to really exceptional talent equipped with total ruthlessness. None of the anti-heroes of the fifties were so qualified.

The Alexandria Quartet

LAWRENCE DURRELL [1957-60]

The four novels which make up this sequence are *Justine, Balthazar, Mountolive* and *Clea.* Durrell terms the work "a four-decker novel whose form is based on the relativity proposition". Pursewarden, one of the characters, tells us what this means. We view life from a necessarily limited angle, but the limitation has nothing to do with psychology, only with the *a priori* facts of time and space. We observe from a given point-instant, but *what* we observe becomes different if we alter our position. "Two paces west and the whole picture is changed."

What this amounts to is that, one novel of the *Quartet* being concerned with time, and the other three with "the three sides of space", we cannot see the whole of any given character or event in one novel alone. Each novel is meaningless on its own, as length or breadth or height or time (which needs space to measure it) is meaningless independently and outside of a mathematics book. *Justine* explains *Balthazar* on one level, while *Clea* explains it on another, deeper, level. *Mountolive* merely keeps time moving. In *Balthazar* Pursewarden commits suicide; in *Mountolive* a reason seems to be given — the conflict between his position in the British Foreign Office and his liking for anti-British Nassim, who is Justine's husband. In *Clea* we discover that he has had an incestuous passion for his blind sister.

It is the exoticism of the setting and the bizarreness of the events which impress the reader more than the somewhat pretentious theorizing about the structure. Anything can happen in Alexandria — pederasty, incest, all the convolutions of lust, all the varieties of betrayal. Enter a teashop, and someone will be screaming in terminal meningitis on the floor above, and the cashier will be suffering ravishment behind her cashdesk, while outside a live camel will be slowly cut to pieces. Durrell's Alexandria is a dream-city caught in prose which seems to emphasize its unreality: "... in autumn the dry, palpitant air, harsh with static electricity, inflaming the body through its light clothing. The flesh coming alive, trying the bars of its prison. A drunken whore walks in a dark street at night, shedding snatches of song like petals. Was it in this that Anthony heard the heart-numbing strains of the great music which persuaded him to surrender for ever to the city he loved?"

The London Novels

COLIN MACINNES [1957-60]

This trilogy — *City of Spades, Mr Love and Justice* and *Absolute Beginners* — is a kind of saga of the displaced, downtrodden or misunderstood. Though the ambience is mostly urban and squalid, there is no attempt, in the manner of "popular" fiction, to exploit the sordid or the violent. *Mr Love and Justice* shows what the world of the prostitute and the ponce is really like, and it examines the conventional image of an incorrupt British police force. *Absolute Beginners* is sympathetic to teen-age culture: inevitably, since rapid change is the essence of it, this culture must seem now somewhat dated. *City of Spades* deals with the condition of West Indian blacks in a London which, in the fifties, was intolerant of racial minorities. MacInnes's books are restrained in their indignation: his blacks are neither brutish, quaint nor innocent, and his whites on the fringe of society are not merely the victims of environment. His characters are not exemplary puppets: they all have free will. As a homosexual who sought "rough trade", MacInnes knew the underside of London life and conveys its atmosphere with authority. He does not, alas, possess a sharp ear for dialogue and, being unable to record faithfully the idioms of the streets, he tends to invent. This is perhaps no fault; the trilogy soars above the condition of a mere journalistic record. It is psychologically accurate, very enlightening, and full of unsentimental compassion.

The Assistant

BERNARD MALAMUD [1957]

Malamud is a remarkably consistent writer who has never produced a mediocre novel. I hesitated between *The Fixer* and *God's Grace* in making my choice of his best work, but *The Fixer* is close to pastiche — it reads like some nineteenth-century Russian novel by an unknown master, superbly translated — and *God's Grace*, with its vision of the end of things in a nuclear war, its talking chimpanzees and the Voice of God, is more of a fable than a novel. Malamud never forgets that he is an American Jew, and he is at his best when posing the situation of the Jew in urban American society. Like Isaac Bashevis Singer, who writes in Yiddish, he is drawn to the older Yiddish literature, in which, without surprise, we see the supernatural — sometimes disguised as surrealism — closing in, the world of objects dissolving, the very identities of people becoming unsure. In *The Assistant* we seem to be assisting at a miraculous conversion. The setting is a New York slum full of very poor Jews. A *goy* hoodlum beats up a grocer, Morris Bober, but is touched by remorse when Bober's injuries prevent his carrying on his business. The remorse is minimal and does not lead to a positive desire to become a good man. He backslides, he remains himself, but somehow the workings of what we can only call divine grace leads him to a new life signalized by his becoming an orthodox Jew, complete with circumcision. The new life, the road to a kind of sainthood, is approached, as always in Malamud, in terms of irony and naturalism: this writer is devoid of either conventional piety or sentimentality. He is always profoundly convincing.

The Bell

IRIS MURDOCH [1958]

This is what Iris Murdoch's earlier fiction was working towards — a synthesis of the traditional and the revolutionary. *Under the Net*, her first, looked like an anti-novel, and *The Flight from the Enchanter* was highly systematized and somewhat artificial. *The Sandcastle*, despite its overlays of symbolism, read much more like a conventional novel. *The Bell* is thoroughly realistic and yet crammed with symbols which sit easily within the plot. The most potent of these is the bell of the title. This is named for the Archangel Gabriel and it is inscribed *Ego Vox Sum Amoris*; it lies drowned in a lake in the grounds of a convent, the legend being that it got there miraculously. It is the still centre of a complex of human problems, the chief of which is summed up in the character of Michael Meade, the founder of a lay religious community on the family estate, where the convent also is situated. Meade has suffered a conflict between his homosexual tendencies and his desire to become a priest; the community he has founded is intended to be a way out of the conflict, a compromise and a compensation, but he learns the truth of the maxim: "to leave the world is not to leave the temptations of the world." There are other characters, all faced with the need to probe the limits of personal morality, to ponder the best means of ordering one's life — by abiding by essential rules or following the *Under the Net* way of existential living, so that one is ruled by "the situation itself". Dora and Toby, intruders into the community, are impelled to drag the bell out of the lake and then to ring it: it is the voice of love, but it is also the cast metal of self-realisation. It is more besides, since it is not in the nature of a poetic symbol to be capable of easy interpretation: there are levels of unconscious myth and magic to which it appeals. This is an intensely poetic novel and beautifully organized.

Saturday Night and Sunday Morning

ALAN SILLITOE [1958]

This novel is another product of the spirit of revolt that animated post-war British fiction. We are hearing, as in Amis's *Lucky Jim*, the voice of the English provinces, and this book may be regarded as a rare example of genuine proletarian fiction. The young hero is a highly paid factory worker: he has more beer and cigarettes than Amis's Jim Dixon will ever see. But he feels that his own comparative affluence emphasizes all the more the injustices done to his class in the past. And the streets of working-class Nottingham are still not very pretty — inadequate sanitation and too many families to a house. Revolt continues to be a virtue: the deserting soldier, one of the hero's family, is considered to have done something heroic. Sillitoe catches the grumbling and the touchiness, the traditional radicalism, the beer, fights, fornication and skittles in a novel whose form is imperfect but whose dialogue is very much alive. For perfection of form one has to turn to the short story *The Loneliness of the Long-Distance Runner*, the title-story of a remarkable volume in which we learn what makes juvenile delinquents tick. Sillitoe, like another Nottinghamshire novelist, D.H. Lawrence, is good at conveying the freshness of life, the poetry of the body, the poetry of the family, the snug human community. But he can be verbose and sprawling, undisciplined. The vitality of *Saturday Night and Sunday Morning* compensates for its faults of form.

The Once and Future King

T.H. WHITE [1958]

White has been ignored in histories of the modern novel, probably on the grounds that he is essentially a fabulist. Certainly the tetralogy — *The Sword in the Stone, The Queen of Air and Darkness, The Ill-Made Knight* and *The Candle in the Wind* — is based on the most enduring British fable, that of King Arthur and his knights, and the approach is closer to fairy tale than, say, Tennyson's Arthurian cycle, but (while Walt Disney's *The Sword in the Stone* stresses the magic) the stage and film musical *Camelot* convinced many that here was a story of real people. I insist that this ambitious work is a true novel, with rounded characters, credible events, and realistic dialogue.

In the first segment White has schoolboyish fun with the boy Arthur under Merlin's tutelage. There is deliberate anachronism: knights of the dark ages speak like this: "You don't say he's comin' down to hunt with those demned hounds of his or anythin' like that?" and there is port after dinner (a disguise for mead) and talk of Eton and Harrow. White's aim is, in a sense, to unscramble the fabulous and bring the story closer to our own time. In *The Queen of Air and Darkness* the anachronisms are very bold, and Merlin says: "The link between Norman warfare and Victorian fox-hunting is perfect." But the story of King Arthur's campaigns is scholarly enough, and Lancelot — the Chevalier Mal Fet — is well-drawn and attractive. His adultery with Guenever is presented delicately, tenderly, but with a quiet undercurrent of necessary guilt. When, at the end of the story, it is "Lancelot's fate and Guenever's to take the tonsure and the veil, while Mordred must be slain", we hear from Arthur's unspoken thoughts a message for our own age — a curse on nationalism. "Countries would have to become counties — but counties which could keep their own culture and local laws. The imaginary lines on the earth's surface only needed to be unimagined. The airborne birds skipped them by nature." Man has to learn to be a better animal. This is not remote and fabulous history: the lesson of the breaking of the Round Table is for our time.

The Mansion

WILLIAM FAULKNER [1959]

Faulkner wrote about nothing but the American South, and he very nearly wrote about nothing but an invented region of that South — Yoknapatawpha County, Mississippi. His long dense sequence of highly idiosyncratic novels ends with the so-called Snopes trilogy, of which *The Mansion* is the last element and the last book that Faulkner wrote. The Snopeses are poor whites, victims of injustice as well as their own native shiftlessness, but tough where the aristocratic families of the Compsons and Sutpens are weak. Mink Snopes sums up the dimly-sensed philosophy of his whole clan in *The Mansion*: "He meant, simply, that *them — they — it*, whichever and whatever you wanted to call it, who represented a simple fundamental justice and equity in human affairs, or else a man might just as well quit; the *they, them, it*, call them what you like, which simply would not, could not, harass and harry a man for ever without some day, at some moment, letting him get his own and equal licks back in return."

Sometimes the reader grows tired of the tough repetitive monologues and the revelations of Southern decay, but in Faulkner there is a massiveness and even a majesty not easily found elsewhere in the American fiction of this century. Mink Snopes, lowest of poor whites — "that had had to spend so much of his life having unnecessary bother and trouble" — at least sees something of human glory at the end of the chronicle: "... the beautiful, the splendid, the proud and the brave, right up to the very top itself among the shining phantoms and dreams which are the milestones of the long human recording — Helen and the bishops, the kings and the unhomed angels, the scornful and graceless seraphim." Turgid and difficult as he is, Faulkner is worth the trouble.

Goldfinger

IAN FLEMING [1959]

Guardians of the good name of the novel (some of them, anyway) may be shocked at this inclusion. But Fleming raised the standard of the popular story of espionage through good writing — a heightened journalistic style -- and the creation of a government agent — James Bond, 007 — who is sufficiently complicated to compel our interest over a whole series of adventures. A patriotic lecher with a tinge of Scottish puritanism in him, a gourmand and amateur of vodka martinis, a smoker of strong tobacco who does not lose his wind, he is pitted against impossible villains, enemies of democracy, megalomaniacs. Auric Goldfinger is the most extravagant of these. He plans to rob Fort Knox of its fifteen billion dollars worth of gold, modestly calling the enterprise Operation Grand Slam, proposing to poison the Fort Knox water supply with "the most powerful of the Trilone group of nerve poisons", then — with the aid of the six main American criminal groups (one of which is lesbian and headed by Pussy Galore) — to smash the vault doors with a stolen Corporal tactical nuclear missile, load the gold on to a Russian cruiser waiting off the coast of Virginia, and, presumably, concoct further villainies in opulent seclusion. Meanwhile the American forces of law and order are supposed to let all this happen. James Bond foils Goldfinger, delesbianizes Pussy Galore, and regards his impossible success as a mere job of work to be laconically approved, with reservations, by M, the head of his department. All this is, in some measure, a great joke, but Fleming's passion for plausibility, his own naval intelligence background, and a kind of sincere Manicheism, allied to journalistic efficiency in the management of his récit, make his work rather impressive. The James Bond films, after *From Russia With Love*, stress the fantastic and are inferior entertainment to the books. It is unwise to disparage the well-made popular. There was a time when Conan Doyle was ignored by the literary annalists, even though Sherlock Holmes was evidently one of the great characters of fiction. We must beware of snobbishness.

Facial Justice

L.P. HARTLEY [1960]

England is recovering from World War III. There have been nuclear attacks and society has only recently emerged from skulking in caves. The new state is afflicted with a profound sense of guilt, and every one of its citizens is named after a murderer. Thus the heroine of the narrative has been christened Jael 97. An attempt to formulate a new morality results in an outlawing of envy and the competitive urge. There must be no exceptional beauty, neither in body (which penitential sackcloth covers anyway) nor in face. A girl who feels herself "facially underprivileged" can be fitted with a standard Beta face, neither ugly nor beautiful. Jael 97 is facially overprivileged: her beauty must be reduced to a drab norm. But, like the heroes and heroines of all cacotopian novels, she is an eccentric. Seeing for the first time the west tower of Ely Cathedral, one of the few lofty structures left unflattened by the war, she experiences a transport of ecstasy and wishes to cherish her beauty. Her revolt against the régime results in no brutal reimposition of conformity — only in the persuasions of sweet reason. This is no Orwellian future. It is a world incapable of the dynamic of tyranny. Even the weather is always cool and grey, with no room for either fire or ice. The state motto is "Every valley shall be exalted." This is a brilliant projection of tendencies already apparent in the post-war British welfare state but, because the book lacks the expected horrors of cacotopian fiction, it has met less appreciation than *Nineteen Eighty-Four*. That Hartley was a fine writer with a strong moral sense had already been confirmed by his *Eustace and Hilda* trilogy, where, as is prefigured in the first book of the three, *The Shrimp and the Anemone*, a young man and woman are locked in a dance of death which they are powerless to halt. The anemone Hilda eats the shrimp Eustace: destruction is part of the law of nature. I hesitated to prefer *Facial Justice* to the trilogy, but, on points of imagination and originality of theme, it seems to win.

The Balkan Trilogy

OLIVIA MANNING [1960-65]

The constituent novels of this sequence are *The Great Fortune, The Spoilt City* and *Friends and Heroes*. The trilogy is probably the most important long work of fiction written by a woman since the war. It seems also to be one of the finest records we have of the impact of that war on Europe. Harriet and Guy Pringle are living in Bucharest at the beginning of *The Great Fortune*. Guy is working for a British cultural mission in Rumania. In the first year of the war Harriet (who is the observer though not the narrator: she observes her own noble absurd husband as well as the big public events in which both are caught up) watches the slow collapse of a corrupt and doomed civilization. The observation finds comic, as well as poetic, expression: the Rumanians are drawn with exasperated tenderness and are sometimes caricatured, but they are always real and rounded. In *The Spoilt City* we move towards the occupation of Bucharest by the Germans after the fall of France; in the final volume Harriet and Guy are in Athens, in a fresh centre of disturbance, accompanied thither by a preposterous *émigré* aristocrat, Yakimov, their friend.

The minute and accurate record of the Balkans under stress of war is only one aspect of the trilogy; the other aspect, perhaps more important, is Harriet Pringle's attempt to understand her husband — a process incomplete at the end of *Friends and Heroes*, taken up again in another trilogy (about the Pringles in Egypt) but never resolved. Guy is a complex character, big, cultured, quixotic, vital, often foolish, demanding — indeed, one of the most fully created male leads in contemporary fiction. He needs plenty of space for setting forth and, summing up the variable contradictoriness of man, he balances the Balkan civilizations which are breaking up, though only, as we know, to be remade on new models. He is a sort of civilization in himself.

The Mighty and Their Fall

IVY COMPTON-BURNETT [1961]

Ivy Compton-Burnett's first novel, *Dolores*, appeared as long ago as 1911, but in 1925 she embarked on the highly original series of fictional structures that begins with *Pastors and Masters* and ends with *The Mighty and Their Fall*. Henry Green's titles follow a pattern of accidence, Ivy Compton-Burnett's a pattern of syntax. *Brothers and Sisters, Men and Wives, A House and its Head, Elders and Betters* — so the stream proceeds, all titles reducible to "(Adj) Noun AND (Adj) Noun". The novels themselves are similarly reducible to a single theme — the consequences of the breaking of the more violent of the ten commandments in respectable upper-class homes, the setting always being late Victorian or Edwardian England. There is a kind of trickery, the sense of a formula, but one cannot read just a couple of the novels and think one knows them all: one needs the whole corpus, not just the underlying pattern. The technique is deliberately formal, even stilted. The following comes from *The Mighty and Their Fall*:

> Something depended from Miss Starkie's skirts, of a nature to unravel when pulled, and her pupils were putting a foot on it in turn, and receding as its length increased.
>
> "Miss Starkie, you have suffered a mischance! Some part of your dress is disintegrating. The mischief should be arrested."
>
> Miss Starkie turned, paused and stooped, and set off in another direction.
>
> "Oh, a bush will serve me, Mr Middleton. I can manage in a moment. Why did you not tell me, children?"
>
> "For a reason that is clear," said Hugo. "Some chances do not come again. Sometimes I regret my childhood. But only for light reasons."

The piquancy of this novel, like its predecessors, comes from the tension between the upper-class formality and the nature of desires which, unspoken in real life, are grossly enacted here. There is no limit to the unnaturalness of the crimes committed within the family circle, but there is little sense of shock. As with Greek tragedy, punishment is left to Nemesis, not to British justice. The characters, swollen by formality of speech and great self-regard, have something statuesque about them, like personages in Aeschylus or Sophocles. The author is totally self-effacing, offering no palliation, making no judgement. We never hear her voice, since her prose-style is carefully modelled on the bland cadences of an earlier age (very much earlier — Jane Austen is always coming to mind): it is itself one of the characters in the tragi-comedy. She deliberately narrowed her range, working over the same ground again and again, offering few new surprises. But within her limits she is beyond criticism.

Catch-22

JOSEPH HELLER [1961]

The title is better known than the book and, indeed, has passed into the language. To avoid a thing you have to accept something worse than that thing: that is Catch-22. Heller writes about American airmen on a small Mediterranean island during the Italian campaign of the Second World War, but he does not work in the great American tradition of bitter realism. His approach is satirical but it is also surrealistic, absurd, even lunatic. But the aim is serious enough — to show the mess of war, the victimization of the conscripts, the monstrous egotism of the top brass. The Nazis are not the target, and the ethics of the struggle against an evil system are hardly touched upon. The enemy is on this side of the fence, the high command of a cynical organization that keeps bomber-crews in the air when they are near-dead with exhaustion, the tame psychiatrists accusing the men of "a morbid aversion to dying" and "deep-seated survival anxieties". Here is Catch-22. What is the punishment for cowardice? Death. What is cowardice? The desire to avoid death. There are lesser cynicisms: a mess-officer steals the carbon dioxide capsules from the flyers' Mae Wests to make ice-cream sodas for the officers' mess. A stock letter is sent out to next of kin: "Dear Mrs, Mr, Miss or Mr and Mrs ——: Words cannot express the deep personal grief I experienced when your husband, son, father or brother was killed, wounded, or reported missing in action" (cross out whatever is inapplicable). When an American airman bombs his own base on behalf of the Nazis the mad satire began to turn sour, and the earnest reader may wish to question whether one can in fact write a satirical novel about World War II. But the mythopoeic power of Heller's novel is considerable.

The Fox in the Attic

RICHARD HUGHES [1961]

This novel broke a creative void of twenty-five years. Hughes's literary reputation seemed settled and sealed by *A High Wind in Jamaica* and *In Hazard* — masterly novels about children written for adults. But in 1961 he announced his embarkment on a long historical novel sequence to be entitled *The Human Predicament*, beginning with *The Fox in the Attic*. Alas, the grand design was no more than initiated, but this present novel is a masterpiece in its own right.

The setting is 1923. Its hero, Augustine, opens the action by walking into modern history carrying a dead child on his shoulder. The child represents the past but is also a device to set the story moving: the small Welsh town where Augustine lives blames him for the child's death, so he leaves Britain and goes to Germany. The narrative is now free to enter the stream of post-1918 history from the German angle: its central event is the failed Munich *Putsch*, its chief "public" character is the emergent Adolf Hitler. The viewpoint is that of an as yet uncorrupted innocence, and thus the technique is not far from that of the earlier books. Mastery of narrative, management of situation, rendering of time and place are exceptionally powerful: the atmosphere of the Welsh town is wonderfully caught, and the corrupt adult world is marvellously symbolized in, for instance, the foyer of the big German hotel, with its subtle odours of dyspepsia. Hughes died with his scheme unrealized, but we must be grateful for what we have.

Riders in the Chariot

PATRICK WHITE [1961]

Patrick White is the only Australian Nobel laureate and he will doubtless be the last for many years to come. His compatriots — Hal Porter, Frank Hardy, Dymphna Cusack, others — are bedevilled by a certain colonial provincialism; unusually, White has been able to write about Australia and transcend its wide narrowness. In *Voss* the grumbling big dog of that continent has been tamed into a highly individual artistic vision. In *Riders in the Chariot* we seem to be in the presence of a great universal drama which is set, almost as though by accident, in a New South Wales locale.

It is a bitter work with very full characterizations: an elderly female recluse living in a decayed mansion, drawn to animals and trees and distrustful of humanity; a Jewish intellectual working as an unskilled factory hand, having found a refuge from Nazi oppression but not from guilt over his wife's death; an aborigine who is no comic abo going walkabout but an integrated human being with a passion for art; a Rabelaisian laundress with a huge family and a drunken husband. All these are united by a common vision of the good, secretly symbolized by the chariot of the title: they are all riders in it. Against the vision of good is set the reality of evil. This is most shockingly manifested in the scene where, on the eve of Good Friday, the Jew is mock-crucified by his drunken cobbers. With so uncompromising a subject, one thing set starkly against the other, there is a danger of melodrama and even caricature, and the work sometimes embarrasses with an over-earnestness which reminds us of Dostoevsky when he is not at his best. But at his best White seems to be a contemporary reincarnation of the great Russian. Even where technique seems to fail, there can be no doubt of an almost blinding sincerity.

The Old Men at the Zoo

ANGUS WILSON [1961]

Sir Angus is a naturalist and realist — one who looks back to both Zola and George Eliot — but in this book, unusually, he indulges a large vein of fantasy. The setting is the future (in the last twenty years it has already become the past, but no matter) and the narrative starts with threats of war — a federated Europe growling at isolated Britain. Against this background political wrangling goes on at the London Zoo — how it shall be run, what its future shall be. It is a small enclosed world, but it is an integral part of British culture, and the problems of loyalty experienced by Simon Carter, the secretary of the Zoo, have universal application. With the coming of war the Zoo collapses, and Wilson's naturalism collapses (or, if you wish, is transfigured) into mythical fantasy. The "Twilight of the Gods" setting in which Sir Robert Falcon, the new director of the Zoo, meets his horrible end; the eating of the animals in a time of famine (inevitably, this has a flavour of cannibalism); the proposal on the part of victorious Europe that the vanquished British shall give gladiatorial displays in the Zoo — these go far beyond the scope of ordinary fictional plausibility, but they are brilliantly rendered. The abiding British countryside, a jungle of refuge, is also rendered with close and loving detail. We are in a world of private nightmare, as Dickens often was, but Wilson has the un-Dickensian courage (perhaps learned from Kafka) to let the nightmare take over.

Another Country

JAMES BALDWIN [1962]

This novel presents a kind of underworld of the afflicted — men and women, whites and blacks, heterosexuals and homosexuals. Baldwin, as a black homosexual, knows all about intolerance. *Go Tell It On The Mountain* deals with black bondage, the cleansing of a black family of inherited Christian guilt (the obsession of the preacher father) in order to pursue the struggle for justice; *Giovanni's Room*, with its Paris setting, is chiefly about a tragic homosexual relationship. *Another Country* is of more general import. Baldwin's theme here is that the divisions which society imposes on itself and regards as fundamental categories are of no importance in face of the only things that really count — the establishment of satisfactory human relationships, the pursuit of love. What does it matter if black sleeps with white, or man with man? If our deepest individual needs are satisfied, we are incapable of seeing life in terms of arbitrary divisions. If society grants primacy to these divisions, thus blocking the individual's right to fulfilment, then society must be fought tooth and nail, for society is evil. The intensity with which Baldwin, through the mostly tragic lives of his characters, makes these points is of a kind likely to, and intended to, shock. His verbal technique can be one of extreme violence, a kind of literary rape. But he is capable of an involuted delicacy learned from, of all people, Henry James.

There is a profound conflict within James Baldwin, derived from a hellfire Christian background which saw the black condition as a punishment for sin, a rejection of sin deriving from his own need to accept his homosexuality, and the new black activism which surrounded him when he began to write. He is a novelist who makes us profoundly uneasy.

An Error of Judgement

PAMELA HANSFORD JOHNSON [1962]

The protagonist is a consultant physician who has done fine work and is revered by his patients. But he is aware that he took up medicine only because he is fascinated by pain: his profession could be a means of inflicting it, or at least withholding its palliatives. He abandons his practice and takes up a job with a less ambiguously altruistic purpose — the rehabilitation of juvenile delinquents. But he meets one youth who has committed a sadistic crime of particular ghastliness. He is gleeful about not having been caught, and he is quite ready to commit the same crime again. Like a vet, the doctor "puts down" the young brute with brandy and sleeping tablets. What sort of moral judgement is the reader expected to make? Pamela Hansford Johnson (Lady Snow) does not force us to a decision: she is not writing from any specific ethical or theological viewpoint. She is saying in effect that no judgement can be satisfactory, that life is too complex to be analysed in terms of the penny catechism or the common law. It is very much the task of her kind of novelist to present moral issues nakedly and leave readers with a sense of hopelessness at the difficulty of making any kind of decision at all. Alas, her style is undistinguished, even slipshod, but human concern shines through.

Island

ALDOUS HUXLEY [1962]

As with so much of Huxley's later fiction, one is not sure whether or not to call this book a true novel. It is less concerned with telling a tale than with presenting an attitude to life, it is weak on characterization but strong on talk, crammed with ideas and uncompromisingly intellectual. Huxley shows us an imaginary tropical island where the good life can be cultivated for the simple reason that the limitations and potentialities of man are thoroughly understood. He presents a conspectus of this life, ranging from modes of sexual behaviour to the technique of dying. Nobody is scientifically conditioned to be happy: this new world is really brave. It has learned a great deal from Eastern religion and philosophy, but it is prepared to take the best of Western science, technology and art. The people themselves are a sort of ideal Eurasian race, equipped with fine bodies and Huxleyan brains, and they have read all the books that Huxley has read.

All this sounds like an intellectual game, a hopeless dream in a foundering world, but Huxley was always enough of a realist to know that there is a place for optimism. Indeed, no teacher can be a pessimist, and Huxley was essentially a teacher. In *Island* the good life is eventually destroyed by a brutal, stupid, materialistic young raja who wants to exploit the island's mineral resources. The armoured cars crawl through, the new dictator makes speeches about Progress, Values, Oil, True Spirituality, but "disregarded in the darkness, the fact of enlightenment remained". The mynah birds fly about, crying the word that means enlightenment: "Karuna. Karuna."

For forty years his readers forgave Huxley for turning the novel-form into an intellectual hybrid — the teaching more and more overlaid the proper art of the story-teller. Having lost him, we now find nothing to forgive. No novels more stimulating, exciting or genuinely enlightening came out of the post-Wellsian time. Huxley more than anyone helped to equip the contemporary novel with a brain.

The Golden Notebook

DORIS LESSING [1962]

The heroine is a novelist suffering from "writer's block" (an affliction that her creatrix seems never to have known, judging from the bulk of her output). Instead of attempting a new novel, she fills four notebooks with four kinds of observation, though her preoccupations are twofold — with the Communist movement in the nineteen-thirties (she became a Communist in South Africa because only the Communists seemed to have any "moral energy") and the emergence of the "free woman". She is close to the Martha Quest of Mrs Lessing's pentateuch *Children of Violence* in spirit and ideals, though she is duller and more humourlessly earnest. Her conception of herself as a liberated female leads her to say hard things about male arrogance, stupidity, sexual impotence and incompetence, and her own sexual frustrations (which are, of course, to be blamed on men) fill up a good part of one notebook. She is intelligent, honest, burning with conviction, but — in the manner of the new Women's Liberationists — she lacks tolerance. The four notebooks merge into the single conception of the "Golden Notebook", and we are told that we have, after all, been reading a novel. We are not altogether convinced. There has been too much diversion of aim, too little digestion of deeply held beliefs into something acceptable as a work of art. The crusader's best medium is the manifesto, which is less concerned with aesthetic balance than with didactic hammering.

The Golden Notebook has, with all its faults, significance as the most massive statement made, up to that time, on the position of woman in the modern world. Mrs Lessing, as her other work shows, has spent much energy on other issues — the relationship of black and white, ruled and ruling, in a British dependency (born in Iran, she was raised in Rhodesia); the panacea of socialism in a tormented world; the question (raised also by the psychiatrist R.D. Laing) of what constitutes sanity. The realistic novel has ceased to satisfy her, and she has found it more comfortable to present her view of the world's misery in the form of a kind of elevated science fiction. *The Golden Notebook* presents her essence, however, and ought to be taken as a historical document of some importance.

Pale Fire

VLADIMIR NABOKOV [1962]

This looks like the work of a man who has seen the world and despises it: only the most ingrown scholarship seems to remain. But one must not leave out of account Nabokov's immense humour. *Pale Fire* is both pedantry and a satire on pedantry. The core of the novel is a 999-line poem by an American author, John Shade — a sort of Robert Frost — which consists mainly of a rather moving meditation on the tragic end of the poet's daughter. After Shade's death, a foolish scholar named Kinbote — an exile from the mythical country of Zembla and a visiting professor of Zemblan at Wordsmith College, New Wye, Appalachia — edits this work, providing a preface and a detailed corpus of notes. But Kinbote has an *idée fixe* — the history of his own country — and he believes that Shade's poem is an allegory of this history, with Kinbote himself — fantasized into the deposed King Charles Xavier II — as the hero. The humour — and Nabokov's humour is subtle as well as occasionally brutal — lies in the disparity between the simple truth of the poem and the gross self-exalting hallucinations of its editor.

The interest of *Pale Fire* is perhaps mainly formal — here is a new way of writing a novel, in the form of a text with *apparatus criticus* — but one can see how it satisfies a particular need of Nabokov's. This is the need to collect and exhibit curious fragments of life and nature for their own sake, not as elements in a narrative plot. *Lolita* almost sinks under a weight of detail; *Pale Fire* is deliberately detail and little else. In Nabokov's masterly four-volume translation with notes of Pushkin's *Eugene Onegin*, the scholar can relax in a vast meadow of detail, knowing that the telling of a story has been handed over to someone else: his true joy is the amassing of bits of coloured glass, strangely shaped stones, old customs, weird words. Nabokov was a skilled butterfly-collector. *Pale Fire* is a brilliant confection.

The Girls of Slender Means

MURIEL SPARK [1963]

Muriel Spark is a Catholic convert and already seems to have joined the Church Triumphant. This means that she can look down on human pain and folly with a kind of divine indifference. There are pain and violence in this brief novel, but perhaps they can be excused because they are related to the public outrage of World War II, which has just finished. The setting is the May of Teck Club, founded for the girls of the title by the late Queen Mary while she was still Princess of Teck. The year is 1945. An unexploded bomb is said to lie buried in the garden, but as this tale is constantly being related by an old spinster with her share of eccentricities, no one takes much notice. Yet the girls themselves are eccentric: Pauline Fox has an imaginary weekly dinner with a famous actor; Jane Wright sends, with no hope of answer, letters to distinguished writers; Selina Redwood carries on a love affair on the next-door roof; Joanna Childe, disappointed in love, recites (with exquisite appropriateness, considering the year), Hopkins's poem "The Wreck of the Deutschland". Even the men in the girls' lives are haunted, one by fear of wire-tapping, another by his work in progress, *The Sabbath Notebooks*. And yet we can accept these strange people as making up a world like our own, since the world that has dropped an atom bomb in its own garden cannot really be accounted sane. Eventually the bomb in the hostel grounds goes off, dealing out wholesale death and destroying the club which is a symbol of human society. But the organization of the story is too subtle for simple allegory: we learn not merely of a phase of world history but of the whole human condition. Muriel Spark, safe with her theological certainties, withholds compassion: as Joanna Childe starts to burn to death, the author chooses this moment for a detailed description of the clothes the poor girl is wearing. Brilliant, brittle, the production of a fine brain and a superior craft.

The Spire

WILLIAM GOLDING [1964]

The best-known novel of Golding is *Lord of the Flies,* which probably earned him his Nobel wreath, but it is a little too systematized and allegorical to be regarded as a true novel. Both *The Inheritors* and *Pincher Martin* seem to be illustrations of a thesis (the essential evil of homo sapiens) rather than representations of human character and action. They disturb not because of their implied moral — man will always choose to destroy if he can — but because this moral is not set in any theological context and because the visions of depravity are not tempered by any apparent love of the depraved. *The Spire* comes closest to being a novel in the true sense: the characters interest us rather more than the revelation of the primacy of evil which, this being Golding, has to be there.

Especially interesting is Jocelin, the dean of a medieval cathedral which seems to have affinities with that of Salisbury. He has a vision of a four-hundred-foot spire erected to the divine glory. But is this vision really derived from God, and is the motive one of pure worship? The addition of the spire to the cathedral involves the commission of more acts of evil than seems proper for an innocent human undertaking. Is the devil behind it? The spire itself is an "unruly member", and the model of the spire becomes an instrument of phallic foolery. The cathedral becomes the scene of sexual enormities and pagan rites. Jocelin himself falls into the sin of lust; the money he acquires for the erection (dangerous word) is from a corrupt source; finally the whole work seems to be founded on a pit of human filth. The dying Jocelin says: "There is no innocent work. God only knows where God may be." Yet the spire is completed, though the vision may not have been innocent, and it thrusts into the sky to the divine glory. Perhaps because of the ecclesiastical context, Golding seems here to have given his revelation of human evil a setting not too far from the theological: the Lord of the Flies, or one of his companion devils, has a place in God's scheme. But of God we know nothing, and of the mystery of evil we have no understanding at all.

Heartland

WILSON HARRIS [1964]

Harris has produced a remarkable Guianan tetralogy — *Palace of the Peacock, The Far Journey of Oudin, The Whole Armour* and *The Secret Ladder* — in which dense and poetic prose serves the theme of the invasion of nature by science and technology. In *Heartland*, with immense economy, he shows the confrontation of logic and magic. Stevenson comes with his machinery to exploit the natural resources of up-river Guiana and is profoundly disturbed by an ancient world he cannot understand and so fears. The mysteries of the jungle are the mysteries of man's unconscious mind. Prose narrative gives out, incapable of further articulation, to match Stevenson's disappearance "somewhere in the Guianan/Venezuelan/Brazilian jungles that lie between the headwaters of the Cuyani and Potaro rivers". All we are left with is a handful of fragmentary poems "so browned by fire that some of the lines were indistinguishable":

> ... world-creating jungle
> travels eternity to season. Not an individual artifice — this living moment
> this tide
> this paradoxical stream and stillness rousing reflection.
> This living jungle is too filled with voices
> not to be aware of collectivity
> and too swift with unseen wings
> to capture certainty.
> Branches against the sky tender to heaven the utter beauty
> ... storehouse of heaven

Harris has the courage to realize the impossibility of conveying, with the ordinary devices of the prose-novel, states of mind corresponding to the horror and grandeur of primeval nature. His own work is on the border between logic and magic. He is probably the best of the Caribbean novelists.

A Single Man

CHRISTOPHER ISHERWOOD [1964]

This is an American novel in that it was written by Isherwood after he had taken US nationality. American critics felt that it was a British novel. One could spend many pages pondering what makes a book with an American setting specifically British. The hero George? He has an English background, but he is as much a naturalized American as his creator (whom he much resembles). It must be something to do with the style — delicate, elusive and allusive, unbrutal, not like Mailer. I do not like the division of the novel in English into national entities. This is a fine brief novel in the Anglophone tradition, whatever that means.

A Single Man has been termed a novel of the homosexual subculture. George has known a long loving attachment to a man who is now dead. He lives alone and we are given a day in his life. He is fifty-eight, a lecturer in a Californian college (we see him teaching, very amusingly, Huxley's *After Many a Summer*). He is charming, liberal, a not very vocal upholder of minority rights. His own homosexuality is subsumed in other assailed minority situations. He tells his students that "a minority is only thought of as a minority when it constitutes some kind of threat to the majority, real or imaginary. And no threat is ever *quite* imaginary ... minorities are people; *people*, not angels." But he seems a threat to nobody — withdrawn, refined, out of sympathy with American philistinism and brashness, a man who has lost his real reason for living. He belongs to that majority (or is it a minority?) called the living, and living means getting through the day. His day is absorbing to the reader, though nothing really happens. He ends up drunk in bed, masturbating. He has a lively vision of death — remarkably described: the silting up of the arteries, the tired heart, the lights of consciousness starting to go out. He goes to sleep; the day is over. To make us fascinated with the everyday non-events of an ordinary life was Joyce's great achievement. But here there are no Joycean tricks to exalt mock-epically the banal. It is a fine piece of plain writing which haunts the memory.

The Defence

VLADIMIR NABOKOV [1964]

This is a worked-over version of *Zashchita Luzhina* ("Luzhin's Defence") — first published in Russian (though not of course in the Soviet Union) in 1930. Before turning to English and becoming one of its greatest modern masters, Nabokov always wrote for an émigré Russian audience. This novel is a typical expression of his somewhat despairing philosophy. As P.N. Furbank puts it, "the only alternative to perversity, with its magical and terrible privileges, is banality." The hero is a chess-player of the master class who can find only two approaches to life — the way of the jigsaw, fitting the shapeless scraps of the world together into a pre-ordained pattern, and the way of chess, the perverse self-absorption in closed-in skills and strategies. His obsession with chess is as much an unclean thing (the way of the jigsaw is the sane way, everybody's way) as Humbert Humbert's obsession with the young girl in *Lolita* (a much inferior novel). If you reject banality — as most of Nabokov's heroes have to — you have to accept the punishment of perversity. When Luzhin has suffered a nervous breakdown he finds no rehabilitation possible, since the obsession which caused the breakdown is his only possible way of life. He throws himself out of a window and, as he falls, sees the chessboard pattern of the windows of the building. He sees also "exactly what kind of eternity was obligingly and inexorably spread out before him".

The style is dense and allusive, the intelligence vast. *Lolita* was a best-seller because of its theme — a perverseness which lubricious readers gloated over while missing the beauty and intricacy of the writing. *The Defence*, less regarded, is more metaphysical and more typical of Nabokov's large talent.

Late Call

ANGUS WILSON [1964]

This may be considered, among other things, to be a study of the New Town. Sylvia Calvert, fat and suffering from high blood pressure, has to retire from hotel management and, with her husband — a ranker officer of the First World War who subsists on anecdotes of his past, grumbles about the present, loans and bets on horses — she goes to live with her widower son Harold, a secondary modern headmaster and pillar of New Town society. Wilson's aim seems partly to show the rootlessness of a community which has opted out of the old values — both rural and civic. Of the vicar of the New Town church — which, inevitably, does not look like a church — Harold says: "You never get any of this dry-as-dust theological stuff from him that's done so much to keep people out of the churches. Quite the contrary. Last Easter he gave a sermon on the eleven plus." The New Town, apparently, would be better for some of that dry-as-dust theology.

What is there for Sylvia Calvert in this community of liberal ideals and bowling-alleys? There is escape into television and the odd nice historical novel from the public library, but the only true release is into country as yet untamed by the New Town, where a farm cat slinks by with a half-dead rabbit in its mouth and a tree is struck by lightning. This, whether we like it or not, is reality. It is the concern with the terrifying and exalting essences underlying the *TV Times*, the drama club committee meeting and the kitchen crammed with gadgets that gives this novel power. Wilson makes no judgements, but, frightening as life can be, he is on the side of life. His eye catches the surface of the contemporary world with marvellous accuracy, but he is not afraid to descend into the dark mines of the human spirit.

The Lockwood Concern

JOHN O'HARA [1965]

O'Hara has never been taken as seriously by his readers as he took himself. He thought of himself as a candidate for the Nobel Prize, but his work tends to carelessness, and his obsession with the world of the wealthy (forgivable enough in a man who rose out of obscure poverty) is considered repellent. But *The Lockwood Concern*, which O'Hara called "an old-fashioned morality novel", transcends both the author's declared intention and the somewhat melodramatic plot. It deals with a Pennsylvania family which becomes wealthy through violence. The founder, Moses Lockwood, kills a robber breaking into his house, shoots a man in the street he thinks to be a vengeful debtor out to kill him. He is impulsive rather than thoughtful and he passes this trait on. O'Hara concentrates on George Lockwood, born in 1873, the third generation, who has seen the family fortune built on blood and confirmed through cold-blooded marriages. He boasts at the end of the book of "the brute force known as the almighty dollar. And there was never anyone here that dared to oppose us." The Lockwoods are ostracised by the society by which they wish to be accepted (only to dominate it): they are brutal, their origins are low. This results in both greater family solidarity and an increase in a kind of hedonistic cynicism. Nemesis steps in. George Lockwood dies by falling down a secret staircase he has had installed in his fine big house (surrounded by a high spiked wall): O'Hara was conscious of the symbolism of this and called it an "instrument of retribution". The book looks, on the surface, like a highly contrived melodrama, but there is a good deal of complexity in it. If George Lockwood is a monster, he is the kind of monster who exhibits the vitality without which America could hardly survive. The rise of the rich is emblematic of the forming of human values which, in America, depend on impulse and energy. O'Hara's women characters are always credible: more than any writer of his time he knew the ruthlessness and the sexual appetites hidden under the show of softness.

The Mandelbaum Gate

MURIEL SPARK [1965]

Muriel Spark must have considered that she was not doing full justice to her talents by exercising it only in small fictional forms. This, however, is her only attempt at a fullsize novel. The theme and the setting are alike promising. The heroine is half-Jewish and half British county family, and she has been converted to Catholicism (this is the author's own position). She goes to Jerusalem to make a pilgrimage to the holy places, but Israel and Jordan share Jerusalem between them, snarling at each other through the Mandelbaum Gate which divides them. Barbara, the heroine, will be in danger in Jordan, since it must leak out that she has Jewish blood, and the plot concerns the attempt of an ineffectual British consular official to get her safely back to the Israeli sector. Much of the story is fantastic thriller material, involving mad disguises, unexpected sexual exploits, discoveries of unsuspected espionage. The moral seems to be that in a mad world — which a divided Jerusalem well enough symbolizes — we must become mad ourselves, throwing away our traditional allegiance to logic. Even the Catholic Church has its contradictions and divisions (as we see, for instance, from the attitude of the Italian Franciscans to the English priest saying mass in the Church of the Holy Sepulchre), but there is eternal truth — Jerusalem the Golden — underlying all. The best analogue of a God who reveals himself in strange ways is the wayward imagination of man. Though there is a certain lack of the old ruthlessness and magic here (it was recovered when Muriel Spark reverted to short forms), it is a well-wrought and stimulating novel hard to forget.

A Man of the People

CHINUA ACHEBE [1966]

The English-language novelists of Nigeria have done much to fertilize standard literary English with the rhythms and idioms of native dialects — Amos Tutuola, for instance, in *The Palm-Wine Drinkard*; Cyprian Ekwensi with *Jagua Nana*; Onuora Nzekwu with *Blade Among the Boys*. Achebe, an Eastern Nigerian, has a persistent theme — the threat of western modes of corruption to native civilizations which the great world may call primitive but are in fact vital and happy. After *Things Fall Apart, No Longer at Ease* and *Arrow of God* he produced in *A Man of the People* a bitter yet funny satire on the personality cult which hides inefficiency and corruption in so many newly independent African states. Here is an example of his idiom:

> ... I do honestly believe that in the fat-dripping, gummy, eat-and-let-eat régime just ended — a régime which inspired the common saying that a man could only be sure of what he had put away safely in his gut or, in language even more suited to the times: "you chop, me self I chop, palaver finish"; a régime in which you saw a fellow cursed in the morning for stealing a blind man's stick and later in the evening saw him again mounting the altar of the new shrine in the presence of all the people to whisper into the ear of the chief celebrant — in such a régime, I say, you died a good death if your life had inspired someone to come forward and shoot your murderer in the chest — without asking to be paid.

Chinua Achebe hits hard. He does not make the error of assuming that evil is a monopoly of white civilization. All power corrupts. He qualifies his acerbity with a compassion for ordinary people which is unsentimental and clear-eyed. He conveys the physical atmosphere of Nigerian town life with sharp economy. This is probably the best book to come out of West Africa.

The Anti-Death League

KINGSLEY AMIS [1966]

This can be described as a masque of ultimate bitterness — not against human institutions but against God — in the form of a secret-weapon-and-spy story. The setting is not the land of the Flemings (though, as Amis's James Bond pastiche *Colonel Sun* shows, he can be comfortable enough in that country) but England in the sixties, with a cold war and a yellow peril, the chief male interest distributed among the officers of No.6 Headquarters Administration Battalion, which is engaged on something secret. This army unit has, as it must have, collective death in view. Someone unknown — we find out at last, but we are expertly kept guessing — finds, among these potential killers, the organization of the title. Ayscue, the chaplain, is sent an anonymous poem for the unit magazine he is starting, and this is the first shot in a war against God. God speaks in this ode *To a Baby Born Without Limbs* and promises "plenty of other stuff up My sleeve — Such as Luekemia and polio" (the misspelling is a deliberate blind).

God is death, the eternal butcher, full of the filthiest and most ingenious practical jokes. The young officer Churchill falls in love with Catharine Casement, who deserves this benison after a nightmare life with a sadistic husband; then God sneaks in sniggering with the gift of cancer to the breast. There are other divinely dealt nastinesses. Ayscue, who says that he took clerical orders the better to wage war on God, risks a prayer towards the end of the story: "Catharine. Don't do it to her. Let her get well and stay well. Please." But, an earnest of His infinite badness, God at once has a stab, not at Catharine, but at a smaller and more defenceless life. I can think of only one sourer ending — that of Graham Greene's *Brighton Rock*, a book which, affirming the devil, also affirms a beneficent God. In this Amis universe there is only God the Great Gangster. Can one really wage war against him? One can make certain existential gestures, totally impotent, but that perhaps is better than doing nothing. Theologically unsound, *The Anti-Death League* is nevertheless a noble cry from the heart on behalf of human suffering.

Giles Goat-Boy

JOHN BARTH [1966]

This book is allegory, parody, didactic treatise, fable, religious codex, and the taking of it seriously entails the taking of it unseriously. Before you begin the story, you have to read a series of fake publisher's readers' reports on the book itself (an ironic frame, as with *Don Quixote*). Then you dive into an all too intelligible allegory. George the hero has been brought up among goats by a Professor Spielman who, out of love with the world which suicidally perverts pure science, has become a tragophile, believing that "der goats is humaner than der men, and der men is goatisher than der goats". George goes to New Tammany College to learn to be human. This is the most important establishment on West Campus, which is in rivalry with East Campus. There have been terrible riots, but none since Tammany invented WESCAC to destroy its enemies. The university is a universe of deadly acronyms. WESCAC can EAT people (Electroencephalic Amplification and Transmission); it has been turned, because of the dangers from EASCAC, into a computer-annihilator of great power. George himself is a product of a Grand-tutorial Ideal: Laboratory Eugenical Selection — hence GILES. His striving towards being a messiah or Grand Tutor gives the book its plot. He rejects NOCTIS (Non-Conceptual Thinking and Intuitional Synthesis), even science itself, and — we have to have a full-length parody of *Oedipus Tyrannos* to make the point — the Panglossian optimism of the Chancellor which, being untragic, is also not tragoid (or goatish). This sounds fantastic and is, all 742 pages of it.

This has to be read as an example of the kind of novel that American professors are capable of producing, seeing the campus as the world and, being free of the marketplace which oppresses non-university novelists, cherishing the paid leisure which can produce really long books on the old pattern of Fielding and Dickens. I was undecided as to whether to give this slot to *Giles Goat-Boy* or to Barth's *The Sot-Weed Factor*, an immense spoof history of early Maryland. Both works extend the scope of the novel — or rather remind it of a scope it has lost, along with a whimsical fantasticality best exemplified in Laurence Sterne's *Tristram Shandy*. Whatever you may think of him, you cannot ignore John Barth.

The Late Bourgeois World

NADINE GORDIMER [1966]

This is a brief taut masterpiece dealing with the realities of life in present-day South Africa. One morning Liz van den Sandt receives a telegram saying that her former husband, Max, has drowned himself. Why? Intelligent, sensitive, a little neurotic, he had wished to live life honourably, not in the manner of the majority of white South Africans, who accept *apartheid* as a condition of their smug prosperity. He had the opportunity of entering one of the professions of the white establishment, or of following a political career like his father's — one that was based on hypocrisy and lies, the alternative being treason to the state. Max rejected such ambition, but the rejection obviated the fulfilment of a need that all human beings have — to belong to the society into which one is born, to be accepted. He sought to be accepted by liberal or radical groups, he even worked with black politicians, but he could not *belong* to the oppressed — the segregated townships, the chained prisoners. Under police interrogation he was forced to betray his white and black associates, totally lost self-respect, had no alternative to suicide.

Liz tells his story and also her own in a South Africa which forced a good man to die and screws her own moral situation to the limit. She lives also vicariously in a hopeful past that is gone, represented by her grandmother, the daughter of a colleague of Cecil Rhodes. She has a white liberal lover and is drawn to a black revolutionary who urges her to burn her bridges, make an end of compromise. The book ends with her lying awake, listening to her heart beat the rhythm "afraid, alive, afraid, alive, afraid, alive...". This is not a propagandist novel, there is no political posturing; it is a study of the crisis whose coming all white South African liberals know cannot be much longer delayed. Lies and oppression cannot go on for ever; meanwhile some men and women are driven to the edge of self-destruction. 160 brief pages sum up the South African disease.

The Last Gentleman

WALKER PERCY [1966]

Walker Percy is a novelist of the American South, perhaps not well known in Britain. James Dickey the poet says: "I consider Mr Percy the most original novelist now writing in English," a large claim. Of the originality one need be in no doubt. The chief character here is a young Southerner, Barrett, decent, amiable, but pathologically withdrawn from life, viewing it through a Tetzlar telescope which, with $8.35, "an old frame house, and a defunct plantation", makes up his patrimony. He sets up his telescope in Central Park, Manhattan, and keeps seeing a lady he thinks of as the Handsome Woman, as well as a girl who he learns is called Kitty. He follows them, eavesdrops, thinks he is in love with the girl, moves in the direction of being involved with people again. He is very much a Southerner, capable of spasms of useless hatred for the Union, romantic though trained as an engineer, chivalric, a misfit in brutal New York. Love is confirmed, but what does one do about love? Love means responsibility not only for Kitty but for her brother Jamie, who is slowly dying of an incurable disease. The three move south, looking for a home, an identity. The plot is less important than the delineation of character, the preoccupation with the way people speak and define themselves geographically and historically (Percy is a professional linguist and has written learnedly about language), and the rendering of a composite South ("the localities in Alabama, Mississippi and Louisiana have been deliberately scrambled," says a prefatory note). The death of Jamie is the more moving for the spareness of the language — "Jamie's bowels opened again with the spent schleppen sound of an old man's sphincter" — and the casual nobility of Barrett, "the last gentleman", never embarrasses.

The Vendor of Sweets

R.K. NARAYAN [1967]

Narayan is the best of the Indian writers in English — graceful, economical, realistic but drawn to fantasy, gently humorous — and the fictional territory of Malgudi he has created is perhaps as important a contribution to modern literature as Patrick White's Sarsaparilla or even Hardy's Wessex. He writes so consistently well that it is painful to limit him to a single book, but *The Vendor of Sweets* can be taken as a way into the others. Its hero is Jagan, middle-aged, a widower with a son, the owner of a sweetmeat shop whose products contradict his own dietary philosophy. He is a follower of Gandhi, a vegetarian, a spinner of his own cloth, and a reader of the *Bhagavad Gita*. His son Mali seems to him to be a typical product of the post-partition age — lazy, a wastrel — but he lavishes on him a troubled affection. Mali becomes an entrepreneur on the Western pattern, returning to Malgudi with a half-American wife and a desire to increase India's literary production through a novel-writing machine (shades of *Nineteen Eighty-Four*). This machine is not altogether implausible: it is to have keys for plots, characters, climaxes; it will convert literature into a major industry. The progressive Mali battles comically with the traditionalist Jagan; the son ends in jail and the father in a more than Gandhian seclusion. The life of Malgudi goes on. This life is beautifully caught, and its aromatic centre is the sweetmeat kitchen, with its blasts of ghee, nutmeg and saffron. Jagan says: "I have always resisted the use of essences for flavouring or colouring. You can get any flavour from Germany; it is easy to deceive even the most fastidious nowadays." But the fastidious Jagan is not deceived by the synthetic flavour of the new world his son imports: he stands, proudly and pathetically, for old India. This book sums up much of what modern India is about.

The Image Men

J.B. PRIESTLEY [1968]

Acknowledged as a competent popular playwright and a decidedly lowbrow novelist, Priestley has been unfairly treated by the "intellectual" critics. Lively, humane, picaresque, he has been sneered at as "the gasfire Dickens". It seems to me dangerous to ignore a novel like *The Image Men*, a two-volume extravaganza longer than *Bleak House* and not less crammed with characters. Priestley, like Dickens, has a social message: we are living more and more in a world of facile images and less and less in our blood, guts and intelligence. The men of the title are a couple of middle-aged academics, repatriated penniless from posts in obscure places overseas. Helped by the British widow of an American tycoon, they cynically start to exploit the modern mania for "the right image" and persuade a new redbrick university to open a department of imagistics, with themselves in charge. Their brainchild develops its own spurious discipline and terminology, which they proceed to convert to practical use in a commercial enterprise. They are gradually taken seriously — mainly by the people of show-business and politics who are much concerned with selling a profitable image of themselves. What could have been purely satirical gains strength from the plausibility of their concept. At the final climax of the story the two men pretend to quarrel and then separate to set up their own enterprises — one commissioned to create a vote-winning image for the prime minister, the other to do the same thing for the leader of the opposition. The two images created come perilously close together, so that it is hard to tell one from the other — this is good satire. With money in the bank, the two leave the world of the image to establish a humanistic college which will purvey the values fast disappearing in the contemporary world. From this same world the two are happy to take what solace it affords — chiefly good malt whisky and sex. But they also fall in love with decent women and marry them.

This is very much the England of the sixties, but the personages belong to the tradition of fictional caricature which is as old as Fielding and Smollett. It lacks ambiguity, fine writing, the poetic touch, but it is honest, vital, even thoughtful. It is also, which too many admired novels are not, vastly entertaining.

Cocksure

MORDECAI RICHLER [1968]

Richler, a Montreal Jew like Saul Bellow, has elected to be one of the literary voices of Canada, unseduced by the land below the Great Lakes. As cosmopolitan a writer as his fellow countryman Robertson Davies, he has set this, one of the bitterest satires of the post-war age, in the swinging London of the sixties. His hero is a Canadian publisher, a genuine hero of World War II with a Victoria Cross, whose innocence and decency are set upon by the new gods of cynicism and permissiveness. His son goes to a progressive school where children are taught to masturbate in front of the "Little Fibber" juvenile brassière television commercials and where an adaptation of the Marquis de Sade is the school Christmas play. His wife prefers the embraces of his never-washed friend Ziggy to his own hygienic caresses. This friend naturally betrays him, publicizing him as the epitome of uptight reaction. On a television show his heroism is a joke, his rescue of men under fire given a homosexual interpretation. A super-tycoon called the Star Maker, whose body is renewed by transplants from selected victims, seeks his lymph system. Every word he utters is perverted by his enemies into a racist smear. We do not see him die. We even expect his last-minute rescue from the smart forces of evil, but his would-be rescuer is a girl so soaked in film that she converts real life into a series of jump-cuts, assumes she has already saved him, and leaves him to the final comic horror. A thorough gentile, he is presented as the archetypal Jew, the gratuitous victim of persecution. All this sounds grim, but the book is grimly funny. Written in the middle of the swinging sixties, it has a very clear vision of Western moral decay.

Pavane

KEITH ROBERTS [1968]

This was probably the first full-length exercise in the fiction of hypothesis, or alternative history, and, with Kingsley Amis's *The Alteration* (which I have no room to include), still the best. We have to imagine that Queen Elizabeth I was assassinated in 1588, that there was a massacre of English Catholics and Spanish invasion of a land torn and divided. England, restored to the Church of Rome, "deployed her forces in the service of the Popes, smashing the Protestants of the Netherlands, destroying the power of the German city-states in the long-drawn Lutheran wars. The New-worlders of the North American continent remained under the rule of Spain: Cook planted in Australasia the cobalt flag of the throne of Peter."

After a two-page prologue, we find ourselves in England in 1968, but an England still Catholic and technologically backward. There are steam trains, complicated semaphore systems, but there is no electricity. The Inquisition is at its repressive work, the Church's grip is vicelike, but there are signs that rebellion is coming. In a coda to *Pavane* we meet a young American of the future who finds a letter to some extent excusing Roman repression: "the ways of the Church were mysterious, her policies never plain. The Popes knew, as we knew, that given electricity men would be drawn to the atom.... Did she oppress? Did she hang and burn? A little, yes. But there was no Belsen, no Buchenwald. No Passchendaele." The Church possessed the knowledge required for building a technological civilization, but she kept it to herself. But "when she knew dominion had ended, she gave back what all thought she had stolen; the knowledge she was keeping in trust." We can accept that or not as we wish. The virtue of the book lies less in its ideas than in its invention of a modern England that is also medieval: it is a striking work of the imagination.

The French Lieutenant's Woman

JOHN FOWLES [1969]

The setting is Victorian England. The hero is Charles, respectable, well-to-do, thoughtful, progressive. He is engaged to Ernestina, a rich, attractive, but highly conventional girl, but he falls in love with the beautiful, tragic, mysterious Sarah who is known to Lyme Regis (where the action begins) as "the French lieutenant's woman" because of some disreputable but romantic episode in her past life. The situation, that of the amorous triangle, is familiar in fiction. What makes this book highly original is that it has three possible endings, all different. "What happened to Sarah I do not know — whatever it was she never troubled Charles again in person, however long she may have lingered in his memory." That is one ending; another and truer one sends Charles in pursuit of Sarah and the consummation of his love. The novel is very modern in that it admits that fiction is lying and manipulation. A true Victorian novel accepted a kind of covenant with the reader, whereby both reader and writer believed they were engaged in following a record of historical or biographical truth. But today we have learned from Jorge Luis Borges that fiction is play and trickery. A novelist can give his hero red hair in the first chapter, make him bald in the third, restore him to hirsuteness, though this time black, in the fifth.

Fowles does not go so far, but he plays a game in which he pretends that his characters have escaped from his control and have a kind of existential freedom that renders them wayward and unpredictable. The author himself appears, disguised as an old man in a railway compartment, bewildered, not knowing where his personages are. The piquancy lies in the conflict between Victorian convention and the modern view of fiction. The author, when not sitting in that railway compartment, is a contemporary anthropologist who surveys this strange world of a century ago with a kind of fascinated horror, knowing far more about the Victorians than they could possibly know themselves but unable fully to understand them. We have here a highly readable and informative book, compelling, thrilling, erotic, but we are not permitted to relax as if we were reading Dickens or Thackeray. A very modern mind is manipulating us as well as the characters.

Portnoy's Complaint

PHILIP ROTH [1969]

This is the novel which is said to do for masturbation what Melville did for the whale. It certainly completed the breaking of the sexual taboo marked (in Britain, at least) by the removal of legal obstacles to the sale of Lawrence's *Lady Chatterley's Lover*. Alex Portnoy is a Jewish boy living in New Jersey. He is incurably but comically sick, with a complex syndrome of which twisted sexuality is only one aspect. The trouble with him is the debilitating power of his mother, a cannibal ambitious for her son but unwilling to let him order his own life: she sits in his belly like an inoperable cancer. It required great literary skill to make so fierce a theme the occasion for such uproarious comedy. Like this:

> Through a world of matted handkerchiefs and crumpled Kleenex and stained pyjamas, I moved my raw and swollen penis, perpetually in dread that my loathsomeness would be discovered by someone stealing upon me just as I was in the frenzy of dropping my load. Nevertheless, I was wholly incapable of keeping my paws from my dong once it started to climb up my belly. In the middle of a class I would raise a hand to be excused, rush down the corridor to the lavatory, and with ten or fifteen savage strokes, beat off standing up into a urinal. At the Saturday afternoon movie I would leave my friends to go off to the candy machine — and wind up in a distant balcony seat, squirting my seed into the empty wrapper from a Mounds bar.

And so on. Whether Portnoy, or Roth, is being fair to Jewish mothers has been a matter of debate. Kingsley Amis said that there would be fewer Mrs Portnoys if there were fewer Alex Portnoys. Certainly the portrait of the devouring mother is monstrous, as is, in compensation, that of the frenzied whacker off. Since Auschwitz it has been forbidden to present the Jews as people subject to the faults of the rest of humanity. Roth has the courage to wish to show things as he has experienced them, but the exaggerations of *Portnoy's Complaint* have a shrillness which could be considered unwholesome if the book were not so funny. It is very funny.

Bomber

LEN DEIGHTON [1970]

There has to be room in fiction for work whose main function is to bring the dead past back to life less through imaginative speculation than by processing (in this instance electronically: the book could not have been written without a sophisticated retrieval system) historical documents. To some of us the Second World War is memory as well as history, but Deighton was only ten when that war broke out: his achievement is to convince us that he was there in the midst of it, a mature recording eye. In some small areas of interpretation he goes wrong: the class system still bedevilled the fighting forces, but the class divisions in the RAF were not quite so bizarre as he presents them. On the other hand he seems never to make a technical or procedural error when reconstructing a massive bomber raid on Germany in 1943. His characters are sometimes in danger of degenerating into types — the radical sergeant-pilot who has "Joe for King" stencilled on his aircraft, the public-school flying officer with his small mind and large ambitions — but he is never wrong about the nervous and visceral responses to flying a Lancaster. He is accurate too about life in a small town in Germany which, by some colossal mistake of calculation, is mistaken for the industrial target entrusted to the mission and shattered. His Germans, soldiers, flying men and civilians, are as credible as the invented personnel of Warley Fen Airfield. In a more recent novel, *Goodbye Mickey Mouse*, Deighton has dared to depict life on an American airfield in Britain with similar success. In *SS-GB* he presents an England defeated by and ruled by the Nazis — again with great plausibility. Deighton's gift is not Jamesian: he is weak on poetic prose and moral involutions, his technique is more documentary than novelistic. But he represents a new and important strain in contemporary fiction and is to be admired for his courage.

Sweet Dreams

MICHAEL FRAYN [1973]

This is a fantasy presented with disarming lightness of touch and tone which is profounder than it looks. Howard Baker, driving to Highgate, finds himself suddenly in a strange but most attractive megalopolis which is the capital city of Heaven. It is run by Cambridge men and women: God is Freddie Vigars, a distinguished but decent scholar of good family, whose wife Caroline is "a kindly-looking girl with thick white legs and her slip showing". She says that Freddie, or God, is a terrific radical. The food eaten at heavenly parties begins with *taramasalata*, continues with *gigot aux haricots* and ends with apple crumble. Howard is set to work, with a team of awfully decent mountain-designers, on designing the Alps. The world is being made, but the world we know (which is being made) already exists. Selections from *Fiddler on the Roof* are played at receptions to meet God. Other Cambridge men are engaged on putting inspiration into the heads of great poets like Donne and Milton; one is even designing man. Howard ends as a planning assistant to God. "This is our task," he says, as he carves the *gigot*; "to provide the harsh materials on which men's imaginations can be exercised, and to offer, through the cultured and civilized life that we ourselves lead here in the metropolis, some intimations of the world they might envisage." ("Meanwhile," murmurs Miriam Bernstein, "here we all sit waiting for second helpings.")

It is an impossible liberal vision, all too Cambridge. But Frayn, who refrains from comment, who is altogether too charming — like his characters — with his easy-going colloquial prose, is fundamentally grim and sardonic. Cambridge cannot redesign the universe. The dream ends. Still, it might be very pleasant if these awfully nice and intelligent Cantabrians of good family could replace blind chance or grumbling bloody bearded Jehovah. There is no sin here, only liberal errors. Frayn was trained as a philosopher. This is a philosphical novel. It is deceptively tough.

Gravity's Rainbow

THOMAS PYNCHON [1973]

I hesitated between this novel, *V*, and *The Crying of Lot 49* when allotting space to Pynchon. A reading of Paul Fussell's fine book *The Great War and Modern Memory* convinced me that, while the others are brilliant higher games, this work, not as yet widely understood, has a gravity more compelling than the rainbow technique (high colour, symbolism, prose tricks) would seem to imply. The subject of the novel is clearly the British Special Operations Executive (SOE) of the Second World War, housed, as I remember, at 62-64 Baker Street, but here transferred to a former mental hospital on the south-east coast called The White Visitation. To this parodic SOE an American lieutenant, Tyrone Slothrop, is assigned in 1944, his task being to learn to predict the dispersal pattern of the V-2 missiles aimed by the Germans at London. The work brings him into contact with Brigadier Ernest Pudding, the commander of the unit (his name echoes that of the head of SOE — Brigadier Colin Gubbins, MC) and a senile veteran of the Great War. He still lives that war, reminiscing about "the coal boxes in the sky coming straight down on you with a roar ... the drumfire so milky and luminous on his birthday night... what Haig, in the richness of his wit, once said at mess about Lieutenant Sassoon's refusal to fight ... the mud of Flanders gathered into the curd-crumped, mildly jellied textures of human shit, piled, duckboarded, trenches and shell-pocked leagues of shit in all directions...". Pudding engages in fortnightly secret rituals with a Dutch girl attached to the unit, Katje Borgesius, who also plays the allegorical rôle of "Mistress of the Night". These rituals are humiliating and involve coprophagy; classic pornography provides the only possible metaphors for the obscenity of war. This is what the novel is about. Fiction allows at last what was forbidden to the original suffering poets and novelists of 1914-18 — the utmost in obscene description, the limit of masochistic pornography. If *Gravity's Rainbow* is often nauseating it is in a good cause. This is the war book to end them all.

Humboldt's Gift

SAUL BELLOW [1975]

This novel probably confirmed Bellow's fitness for the Nobel Prize. It is in competition with *Herzog* as the best of Bellow's extended fiction, but it has less self-pity in it and is much funnier. The hero-narrator is Charlie Citrine (a name apparently taken, like Moses Herzog, from Joyce's *Ulysses*), a successful but impractical Chicago writer who was a friend of the dead failed poet Von Humboldt Fleisher (probably based on Delmore Schwartz). The gift of the title is a film scenario which, after long incubation, emerges from nowhere and makes Citrine improbably rich. Bellow seems to know little about the film world, but no matter. He knows Chicago very well and much of the book concerns Citrine's comic misfortunes, and rarer triumphs, in that city. He is in trouble with a small vicious gangster improbably named Cantabile, who is drawn to Citrine because of his very apparent inability to cope with the real tough world. He is in trouble with his divorced wife, who demands more alimony. His girl friend, the gorgeous animal Renata, talks of turning into Persephone and marrying a king of the dead, a successful mortician. The story moves slowly, but we do not mind. The richness with which Bellow presents the physical world, into which he allows Citrine's moral and metaphysical speculations to intrude at length, is a great joy. Cirtine's much qualified success as a writer (Pulitzer Prize, ribbon of the *Légion d'honneur*) is contrasted with the decay of Humboldt, who, though dead, will not lie down. The distinction of the book lies, as always with Bellow, in its presentation of character. We do not much care whether his personages labour at furthering the plot: they are a pleasure to contemplate in themselves. Citrine's wealthy capitalist brother, for instance, does nothing except delay Citrine's flight for Spain (Renata does not wait for him there: she goes off with her mortician), but we are happy to be presented with him in depth and breadth. Bellow may be considered not altogether a natural novelist — he rarely moves from Chicago; much of his material is autobiographical — but he excels at animating a distinguished prose style with the pulse of life.

The History Man

MALCOLM BRADBURY [1975]

Two small technical innovations have to be mentioned first. The present tense is used throughout and dialogue is not indented. The traditional mode of making each line of dialogue a separate paragraph has always tended to give too much weight to utterances (like "Yes" and "No") which lack weight. Bradbury's dialogue runs on and on as in real life and, as in real life, everything is immediate and *now*. These devices are in the service of a story of redbrick campus life in the South of England. The protagonist, Howard Kirk, is a lecturer in sociology, which has to mean that he is a radical positivist. Successful, dogmatic, a voice of justice and tolerance — so long as these are not meted out to elements he calls reactionary — he sleeps around with students and colleagues, while his wife Barbara spends weekends with a young actor in London. This is the new graceless world of trends, Conran furniture, permissiveness, radical causes, sit-ins, Jesus jeans. The great virtue of the narrative is that it narrates without making value judgements. A single event at the end — Barbara agonizedly thrusts her bare arm through a window at one of the Kirks' permissive parties — is enough to indicate that this kind of freedom has to be paid for. The crux of the novel is Howard's persecution of a male student whose life-style and political stance he refuses to accept: sociology is a radical discipline unamenable to "reactionary" interpretations. Howard is a detestable character whom most of his students love. The danger of his being fired on grounds of "gross moral turpitude" is obviated by radical yells, posters ("Work for Kirk"), sit-ins. It is a disturbing and accurate picture of campus life in the late sixties and early seventies. Its great aesthetic virtue, apart from the technique which so brilliantly serves physical immediacy, is its total objectivity. No judgement is forced, we make up our own minds. There will be readers capable of seeing Howard Kirk as a personification of all the modern virtues.

The Doctor's Wife

BRIAN MOORE [1976]

Sheila Redden, Irish, Catholic, thirty-eight, a mother, married to a Catholic doctor in Belfast, falls in love with an American twelve years her junior on holiday in Villefranche. The situation is not uncommon in fiction. What is original in this novel is the manner in which the moral dimension of the situation is treated. There was a time when we could make sound ethical and theological judgements on our sexual aberrations (the sex here is wholly candid without touching the pornographic) and allay our frustrations in a sense of duty, but those days are gone. Sheila, sun-drenched on the Côte d'Azur, Pernod-sipping in Paris, cannot cleanse her mind of the Belfast atrocities, which are an expression of religious enmity. God seems no longer around. What we have instead of God is not secular morality but doctrines of mental stability — which Sheila's husband invokes to persuade her that her conviction of love is probably insanity — allied to the blackmail of duty (think about your poor son). Again, how far does the future exist in the present? Is it common sense to think of what the age-gap will look like in ten years time when now it doesn't seem to matter? Sheila's agonies are real, and the paradox of her seeming to be, for the first time in her life, in a state of grace when she is technically sinning has a poignancy which the cool, simple, objective prose does not seek to poeticise. Moore has never written a bad novel, but the moral profundity of this one gives it a rare distinction. It jostles with his most recent — *Cold Heaven* (1983) — for a place here, but I think it prevails.

Falstaff

ROBERT NYE [1976]

François Rabelais presents characters, even though some of them are giants, and events, even though many are implausible, and so may be considered to be a novelist. Joyce was influenced by him, and in many post-Joycean novelists the urge to expand fiction Joyceanly is really a desire to return to Rabelais. Robert Nye has stolen Shakespeare's Falstaff, unrelating him to the historical original, and, as it were, unbuttoned him. He becomes here more than a witty exemplar of gorging and philosophical cowardice; he is turned into a god of fertility. A chapter entitled "About Sir John Falstaff's Prick" is wholly Rabelaisian with its bawdy catalogue, though Rabelais would have gone much further. However much we long to be back with Pantagruel and Panurge, we cannot lose all our inhibitions. Nye is occasionally facetious — "Buckram," Falstaff says to Hal, "becomes you. It goes with your eyes" — but on the whole he combines, very successfully, the forward drive of modern fiction with the wordy divagations of a more monkish tradition. His Falstaff cannot be greater than Shakespeare's, but the whole sprawling portrait is a relevant gloss on Shakespeare as well as a restoration of Falstaff to his true historical context (Shakespeare's Falstaff is a post-Reformation sceptic; Nye's is a backsliding Catholic). And the erotic candour is of our own time:

> The lovely focative sucking over, just this side of emission, she'd let my engine out of her spiced trap — (Mrs Nightwork was a great one for eating garlic and cloves.) Then she'd press my prick to her cheek, which was usually cool as cream. She had a trick of fluttering her eyelashes upon the delicate skin just below the head, where the foreskin puckers, which I found delicious....

This book was a bold venture and an indication of what the novel can do when it frees itself from the constraints of the Jamesian tradition.

How to Save Your Own Life

ERICA JONG [1977]

Erica Jong is primarily a poet, and this novel ends, not implausibly since it is a story about a search for love, with a series of love poems. A concern with putting the right words in the right order is a good quality in a novelist, and Ms Jong beats many of her feminist sisters (Marilyn French, for instance) through real distinction of style. Her first novel, *Fear of Flying*, impressed because it seemed to tell the truth about woman's sexual and emotional needs. Its successor deals with the inner perturbations that accompany literary success — to be glossed as success in reaching the hearts of suffering women, which apparently means all women. *Fear of Flying* has been fictionalised into *Candida Confesses*, and its author suffers the sweet agonies of fame while trying to decide whether or not to leave her husband. "Why is it harder to leave a loveless marriage than a loving one? Because a loveless marriage is born of desperation, while a loving one is born of choice...." The contemporary American scene is painted very sharply, with its psychiatrists and ballyhoo merchants, its bizarre modes of sexual release. Ms Jong has read all the books and sampled all the cuisines and erotic positions, just like her heroine. There is an intensity here which just fails to reach neurosis, and it is always qualified by a strong sense of the ridiculous (consider the scene where a woman can attain orgasm only through being masturbated by a champagne, not a beer, bottle). There is a good deal of wisdom, not all of it grateful to liberated women: let all women, says Ms Jong's heroine, claim their right to orgasm (cognate with the right to colour television) and then let's all get on with the real business of living. This means love.

> They lay not moving in the absolute peace after the earthquake. She felt a small sun glowing in her solar plexus, and her legs and arms too heavy to move, mercury-filled moon suits, leaden limbs. He held her to him even as his cock grew soft and curled away from her. "I'll never leave you," he said, "never."

There is nothing wrong with a happy ending.

Farewell Companions

JAMES PLUNKETT [1977]

Plunkett's first novel, *Strumpet City*, appeared in 1969 and was highly acclaimed. It deals with Dublin in the years preceding the First World War. *Farewell Companions* starts after the war and takes the reader up to the end of the second one. It begins with the Troubles and ends with an Irish view of the bomb that fell on Hiroshima. "O'Sheehan speculated on the possibility of consequential climatic changes on a global scale, involving in the case of Ireland specifically the danger of permanent diversion of the Gulf Stream." O'Sheehan has suffered a head injury in the Troubles. He is convinced that he is Oisin, son of Finn MacCumhaill. When asked if he remembers any earlier military engagements than those of the twenties, he says: "Many of them. I have always resisted the ancient enemy; as a Fenian, as a united man, as a follower of Sarsfield, in fact whenever the opportunity arose. Before the British it was the men from Scandinavia, the Fair Strangers we called them. I resisted them too." O'Sheehan grants Plunkett the dimension of fantasy, of the mythical past existing in the present, that, since Joyce and Flann O'Brien, has been necessary to Irish novelists. O'Sheehan is a personification of Ireland, but the real hero is Tim McDonagh, first taught by nuns, then by the Christian Brothers, brought up on the Virgin Mary and hellfire. He sees the large events of history flowering remotely: Ireland has cut herself off from the world. The lads sing "Ramona" and "Carolina Moon" and, when the time comes, use expressions like "bloody wizard" and talk of joining the British forces in Belfast. ("No longer your home. No longer my son. A renegade.") Tim remains neutral though not patriotic: "Hurricane, famine, earthquake, volcano, even a world war have no real impact. Kathleen née Hoolihawn won't cast a glance beyond her four green fields."

This is an ambitious panorama of Dublin life in a time of change and the resistance of change. It is difficult to write a long Dublin novel since *Ulysses*, but Plunkett has produced an unjoycean work of great architectonic skill which encapsulates vividly the era when Ireland opted out of the world. This is quite an achievement.

Staying On

PAUL SCOTT [1977]

Scott's *Raj Quartet* is a somewhat shapeless monster, over-regarded, despite its being crammed with love and concern for Mother India. This short novel says a great deal about the relationship between the white man and the manumitted brown man and says it very succinctly. Colonel "Tusker" Smalley (Indian Army, Retd.) and his wife Lucy are still living, long years after partition, in a hill-station called Pankot. Things are not what they were. The figure of authority is no longer the visiting Viceroy but the sixteen-stone Mrs Bhoolabjoy, who has bought the hotel where the Smalleys live and banished them to its annexe. Servants are no longer deferential. Ibrahim, who works for the Smalleys, has seen the West as an illegal immigrant (Finsbury Park) and, on British television, even the ends of films his servile duties made him miss at Indian club showings. Colonel Menektara, despite his continued devotion to Raj military English, now gives parties to observe Hindu festivals. "Tusker" is old, liverish, ill, and his death is imminent. Lucy worries about her future, the daughter of an Anglican clergyman who finds it hard to take in the coal-blackness of the Tamil Father Sebastian at the hill-station church, whose Christian friends will have to be Eurasians, who, a widow, ends a mainly comic novel in genuine distress: "Oh, Tusker, Tusker, Tusker, how can you make me stay here by myself while you yourself go home?" This is an admirable panorama of life in the India of 1972, in which the love-hate relationship of rulers and ruled goes on posthumously, the new neutral American West replaces cosy bumbling British patronage, and the author's obsession with that damnable wonderful country finds its best expression.

The Coup

JOHN UPDIKE [1978]

There is an imaginary African territory called Kush (low Arabic, one seems to remember, for the female genitals), landlocked, south of the Sahara, agonized by drought. Its dictator is Colonel Hakim Félix Elleloû, a former soldier of the colonizing French and a student of a small Wisconsin college. He is a Muslim and has the statutory four wives. He is driven round in an air-conditioned silver Mercedes. He rules over a hungry state which officially professes a kind of Islamicized Marxism and houses in bunkers at its borders the *équipe* of a Soviet missile. Hakim detests America but is haunted by it. America generously unlades megatons of junk food for starving Kush, but Hakim scornfully rejects it. But, whether he will or not, American influence creeps in, American know-how prevails, and the consumer revolution is proclaimed. When Hakim goes into exile as a short-order cook, the five-year-awaited rains arrive. He ends in Nice on pension, writing his memoirs in the style of John Updike.

This work is full of poetry, about African landscape in all its aspects, the shoulderblades of women, the refrigerator snack after the hour of love, the gush of blood at the severing of a head, Pepsi and Coca, leather, a fly's flight. There is a large lyric love of the surface of the world, in which accurate visual notation conjoins with a great verbal gift. Ideas abound. Hakim insists that French literature more than French political thought is the colonialist's gift to Africa — the dryness of Ronsard and the ironic hopelessness of Villon. There is perhaps too much intelligence as there is too much eloquence. Updike gives Hakim a too shrewd notion of the impossibility of an Afro-American rapprochement. All those corn flakes and the goats' udders dry. Agricultural miracles, but the grazing grounds cropped to nothing by cattle which forget how to wander. The book is finally a sour-mouthed hymn to the United States, where men are so fat that they jog and cut down on peanut butter — thus impairing Kush's sole export. It is a beautifully written disturbing lyric composition in which the physical world exists.

The Unlimited Dream Company

J.G. BALLARD [1979]

Ballard is known as a writer of science fiction, a term which perhaps has no real validity. If science fiction constitutes a separate genre it demands new rules of appraisal. These not being available, it is proper to think of works like *The Invisible Man*, *The Time Machine* and *The Unlimited Dream Company* as belonging to no new category. They stand or fall as novels. This is perhaps the best novel that Ballard has written. We are in contemporary England. A young man who does not fit well into conformist society steals an aircraft and, not having flown a plane before, crash-lands on the Thames near Shepperton. We do not know whether or not he survives the crash: what follows may be a death or afterlife vision. He is rescued from drowning by a group who have been foretold of his coming as a kind of messianic redeemer. He discovers supernatural powers in himself which lead him to a total transformation of the town. This is isolated from the rest of the world and becomes a place of miraculous happenings — the spontaneous flowering of tropical vegetation, the appearance of strange wild animals. There are pagan fertility festivals and an uninhibited attitude to sexual congress, which is practised openly. "Shepperton had become a life engine." The outside world tries to break in but cannot: "A fireman with a heavy axe began to hack a path through the stout bamboo. Within a dozen steps he was surrounded by fresh shoots and wrist-thick lianas that laced him into the bars of a jungle cage from which he was released only by the winches of the exhausted police." The writing is distinguished and is in the service of an Edenic vision which has its intrusive snakes. When Blake, the hero, feels despair he floods the town with it: Shepperton is an extension of himself. At length the townsfolk take to the air — "fathers, mothers, and their children — our ascending flights swaying across the surface of the earth, benign tornados hanging from the canopy of the universe, celebrating the last marriage of the animate and inanimate, of the living and the dead." It is an apocalyptic book but also very much a novel.

Dubin's Lives

BERNARD MALAMUD [1979]

This, if not quite so magical a book as *The Assistant*, is a haunting study of one aspect of the human condition — not necessarily Jewish, though the protagonist is a Jew. William Dubin is a professional biographer engaged on a life of D.H. Lawrence. He lives with his Gentile wife Kitty in rural Vermont, buckling daily to his difficult task — for he has little in common with his subject — and walking the woods and lanes for relaxation. No novel I know does better at painting the procession of the seasons, the slow turning of year after year. Dubin is in his late fifties and aware that life is passing him by: indeed, Lawrence, dead at forty-five, bullies him with messages about sexual fulfilment. He has a sexual encounter with a young student, Fanny, who is earning an honest buck by doing the Dubins' housework. Pretending to his wife that he is doing Lawrence research, he takes the girl to Venice, where she is visibly unfaithful to him with a gondolier. Enraged, humiliated, thwarted, he goes home but finds the resumption of work difficult. He meets Fanny again and, after some initial reluctance, resumes a secret life with her — trips to New York ostensibly for more research, eventually cohabitation in a barn, almost within earshot of his wife. Middle-aged madness, true, screaming infidelity, lies and subterfuges, the daily paradox of Lawrence's unfaithfulness to Frieda and the Laurentian phallic doctrine, but Dubin is at least and at last living. How can he square his infidelity with his duty to his wife, as well as to his daughter — who has had an affair with a black man even older than Dubin and is pregnant — and to his stepson, who escaped from the Vietnam war to Stockholm and has now been recruited by the KGB? Malamud twists the pain to breaking-point, but always with compassion and bitter humour. This is a novel for middle-aged men, who will all see themselves in Dubin, but it is also a penetrating study of America under Nixon, when lies and hypocrisy had presidential approval. There is no real ending to the book, which is a grave fault. This is life scrupulously rendered, but Malamud is perhaps too honest to give it an artistic shape. Yet shape is the essence of the novel.

A Bend in the River

V.S. NAIPAUL [1979]

Naipaul, a Trinidadian of Indian Brahmin blood, has written magisterially of his own island but has travelled widely — in India, Africa, Iran, South America — to record the human condition, which fills him with little optimism. This novel, his best, has an African setting and it presents, in a small gloomy town on a bend of a great river, a pretty hopeless human prospectus. Salim, whose forbears came from India to settle on Africa's east coast, sets up a small business in the very heart of darkness. The town was formerly an Arab settlement, later rebuilt by Europeans, but the enterprising foreigners have all but disappeared and life is controlled by a corrupt dictator in the distant capital. Political convulsions periodically wipe out the town, but the dour human will to survive rebuilds it. Salim sees that his own fate is to be an isolated individual cut off from any sustaining society, a sad observer whose will to survive alone defines him. His sole companion is Metty, the son of one of the family's slaves, and Salim reflects much on the nature of slavery, an abiding fact of the modern as of the ancient world (nowadays slaves have passports and walk ahead of their mistresses on Bond Street) and sees liberty in very relative terms. The hectoring dictatorial voice on the radio — announcing new privations in pseudo-affectionate big brotherly tones — stands for all political liars. Meanwhile the people suffer, monkeys look as if they know they are going to be eaten, new enterprises spring up only to dry up like plants without nutriment, and the river abides. The story ends with Salim leaving the territory — having found a brief and poignant unity with a transitory mistress — and the guns of the Liberation Army preparing to open fire. But liberation is a hopeless notion. This is a beautifully composed book, with an almost Conradian power of description. Aesthetically most satisfying, it is also profoundly depressing. But depression is sometimes a stone on the road to literary exaltation.

Sophie's Choice

WILLIAM STYRON [1979]

The narrator is a young man from the South — Stingo, a would-be novelist who comes to New York in 1947 and settles with his pencils and pads in the rooming house in Brooklyn. Here he meets Sophie, a Polish Catholic immigrant not long out of Auschwitz, who is living with Nathan, an erratic but brilliant Jewish intellectual. Stingo is drawn to both fascinated at first by the erotic abandon of their life together, while he himself vainly seeks to get laid. He learns in time of Sophie's suffering under the Nazis and is forced into the mature stance of considering the nature of evil. He sees a connection between the now vanished Poland ruled by an intolerant aristocracy and his own American south, whose romantic dreams of chivalry were made possible by the kind of slave economy the Nazis developed. Can the past be wiped out? The concentration camp number is still there on Sophie's arm when she bathes at Coney Island; Stingo's venture into literature is being partly financed by black slave money. Public wrongs are mimicked by private agonies. The unstable Nathan snarls with demented jealousy at Sophie's supposed infidelities: there is always the matter of her family's traditional Polish antisemitism to bring up; he, a Jew, has been cosseted by America, while she, a Gentile, has known all the torments of an enslaved people. The choice she was given at Auschwitz — whether to let her son or her daughter go to the gas chamber — is reserved till the end of the book. The fledgeling writer Stingo says: "Someday I will understand Auschwitz," but realizes the absurdity of the statement. "At Auschwitz, tell me, where was God?" The reply is: "Where was man?" Sophie and Nathan, authors of their own private agony which is a figure of all the wrongs of history, eventually die together, listening to a record of Bach, in a kind of *Liebestod*. Stingo, schooled in man's condition, is ready to become William Styron and write his book about black rebellion — *The Confessions of Nat Turner*.

It was a daring act for Styron, whose sensibilities are wholly Southern, to venture into the territory of the American Jew, to say nothing of his plunge into European history. The book is powerfully moving, despite the Southern tendency to grandiloquence, the decking of his prose with magnolia blossoms where starkness was more in order.

Life in the West

BRIAN ALDISS [1980]

Aldiss is so highly regarded as a practitioner of science fiction that we have to remind ourselves that he is a fine realistic novelist. The Horatio Stubbs series that began with *The Hand-Reared Boy* and anticipated the masturbatory obsession of Alex Portnoy has its own rough virtues, but *Life in the West* is a finely crafted work with a wide social range and a large intellectual content. It concerns Thomas C. Squire, a successful specialist in media theory and practice, now in handsome early middle age and facing the collapse of his marriage, the abandonment of his Georgian mansion, the approaching dissolution of a great family name. We could call the book a novel of mid-life crisis, but it seems better to see Squire's situation as emblematic of that of the West in an age of recession and doubt. "Inflation isn't going to go down.... The Arab world is going to squeeze Europe and the US by the throat.... We're going to go down the drain, till we end up like a lot of little Uruguays and Paraguays...." So says one pessimist, but the life of Squire is based on belief in a future: he has become famous for his advocacy of popular art, whose serious appreciation lies in the future. The very contemporary flavour of this novel lies less in the matter of recording the actualities we know than in its presentation of a paradox we sometimes ignore: while we think the world is collapsing we are surrounded by technological marvels which proclaim hope, and we are faced with the exhilarating task of creating new metaphysical and aesthetic systems which presuppose a fuller richer life yet to be realised. Much of the action takes place at the First International Congress of Intergraphic Criticism in a town in Sicily: here we learn something of the new aesthetics and see how the divided world of international politics seeks to qualify the blessedly pure speculations of the thinker concerned only with the quality of life — the salvatory concrete, not the abstract evil. This is a rich book, not afraid of thought, full of vital dialectic and rounded characters.

Riddley Walker

RUSSELL HOBAN [1980]

"On my naming day when I come 12 I gone front spear and kilt a wyld boar he parbly ben the last wyld pig on the Bundel Downs any how there hadnt ben none for a long time befor him nor I aint lookin to see none agen." So the book begins. It is a dangerous and difficult dialect of Hoban's own invention, but it is altogether appropriate to an as yet unborn England — one that, after a nuclear war, is trying to organize tribal culture after the total destruction of a centralized industrial civilization. The past has been forgotten, and even the art of making fire has to be relearned. The novel is remarkable not only for its language but for its creation of a whole set of rituals, myths and poems. Hoban has built a whole world from scratch. Sometimes these strange English people find the remnants of old machines, but they have forgotten their meaning. "Some of them ther shels ben broak open you cud see girt shyning weals like jynt mil stoans only smoov." The lost past is contained in a kind of sacred book called *The Eusa Story*, whose first chapter is this: "Wen Mr Clevver wuz Big Man uv Inland they had evere thing clevver. They had boats in the ayr & picters on the win & evere thing lyk that. Eusa wuz a noing man vere quik he cud tern his han tu enne thing. He wuz werkin for Mr Clevver wen thayr cum enemes aul roun & maykin Warr. Eusa sed tu Mr Clevver, Now wewl nead masheans uv Warr. Wewl nead boats that go on the water & boats that go in the ayr as wel & wewl nead Berstin Fyr." Finally they make use of "the Littl Shynin Man the Addom he runs in the wud". This novel could not expect to be popular: it is not an easy read like *The Carpetbaggers*. But it seems to me a permanent contribution to literature.

How Far Can You Go?

DAVID LODGE [1980]

Lodge and Malcolm Bradbury are considered to be Britain's outstanding novelists of campus life, but Lodge here steps outside the boundaries of agonized academia and deals with the problems of Catholics in the age of Vatican II. His main concern is Catholic sexual morality, and his title bluntly puts the question which concerns all who cannot reconcile orthodox doctrine with natural urges. University students in the fifties, Lodge's characters become, some of them, parents in the seventies, seeing in bewilderment in the swinging sixties a great secular sexual revolution but finding no doctrinal compromise in the pronouncements of the papacy. But wait. If marital congress is permitted during the so-called "safe period" — the partners playing "Vatican roulette" — does not this really mean the separation of the sexual act from the duty of peopling heaven with human souls? Lodge, unlike Bradbury, puts himself firmly in the scene:

> While I was writing this last chapter, Pope Paul VI died and Pope John Paul I was elected. Before I could type it up, Pope John Paul I had died and been succeeded by John Paul II, the first non-Italian pope for four hundred and fifty years: a Pole, a poet, a philosopher, a linguist, an athlete, a man of the people, a man of destiny, dramatically chosen, instantly popular — but theologically conservative. A changing Church acclaims a Pope who evidently thinks that change has gone far enough. What will happen now? All bets are void, the future is uncertain....

The author joins his characters in being bewildered, decent, doubtful, willing to give allegiance to a Church which seems to have abolished hell but not resolved the basic human problems of its members. A sense of pragmatic British humour is needed, and Lodge, like is own personages, has it. But there is a certain bitterness too, a high moral seriousness underneath the flippancy and accuractely caught atmosphere of middle-class Catholic intellectual England.

A Confederacy of Dunces

JOHN KENNEDY TOOLE [1980]

This novel has a sad history behind it. The author sent it to every publisher in America, all of whom rejected it. After the final rejection (by Knopf) Toole committed suicide. He was only thirty-two. His mother gave the manuscript to Walker Percy, who secured its publication by Louisiana State University Press, and it was awarded a posthumous Pulitzer Prize. Its virtues have now been universally recognized. It is a fine comic extravaganza set in contemporary New Orleans, with an eccentric hero named Ignatius Reilly whose true home is the middle ages and who loathes the modern world. He does more than loathe it — he disrupts it. Forced by his illiterate mother to get a job, he leads a revolt in a pants factory, eats up the stock of a hot-dog merchant, breaks up a nightclub. With the black jivecat Jones, pot-smoking in space-age dark glasses, we have a remarkable reproduction of the very tonalities of New Orleans creole speech:

> Whoa! I never go to school more than two year in my life. My momma out washing other people clothin, ain nobody talkin about school. I spen all my time rollin tire aroun the street. I'm rollin, momma washin, nobody learnin nothin. Shit! Who lookin for a tire roller to give them a job? I end up gainfully employ workin with a bird, got a boss probly sellin Spanish fly to orphan. Ooo-wee.

The importance of a piece of fiction about a particular place can be gauged by the extent to which it modifies our response to the place itself. Dublin has been a changed place since *Ulysses*. New Orleans can never be the same again after Toole's comic masterpiece.

Lanark

ALASDAIR GRAY [1981]

A big and original novel has at last come out of Scotland. Gray is a fantastic writer (and his own fantastic illustrator) who owes something to Kafka but not much. He has created a mythical city called Unthank, a kind of lightless Limbo where people succumb to strange diseases and then are transformed into crabs, leeches, dragons before disappearing without trace. This nonplace has a vague resemblance to contemporary Glasgow. Lanark, one of its citizens, indeed eventually its Provost, suspects that he is a metamorphosis of an earlier life-form, consults the Oracle in a strange place called the Institute and is granted a vision of the life of a young man named Duncan Thaw, growing up in a real Glasgow, preoccupied with the problem of reconciling his artistic ambitions with the maintaining of ordinary human relationships. All this is good traditional naturalism. Thaw dies, and it is not clear whether his death is accidental or suicidal. He finds himself in Unthank, which nightmarishly reproduces aspects of his past life. His identification with Lanark is vague. Lanark sets out now on a mad journey "through the mist and time chaos of the Intercalendrical Zone", visits a city called Provan, where the citizens drink rainbows and are oppressed by security robots. Gray attempts no linguistic innovations, though his footnotes and marginal glosses recall *Finnegans Wake*. Whether his intention is satirical is not clear. It is best to take this novel as the emanation of the fancy of a Celt with a strong visual imagination and great verbal power. Scotland produced, in Hugh MacDiarmid, the greatest poet of the century (or so some believe); it was time Scotland produced a shattering work of fiction in the modern idiom. This is it.

Darconville's Cat

ALEXANDER THEROUX [1981]

This novel will be termed Joycean by some, specifically those who do not find in *Ulysses* the urgency of true fiction. It would be more fitting to relate it to such sports as *Tristram Shandy* and *The Anatomy of Melancholy*. There is also a strong reek of the dictionary, which may be no bad thing in an age when much fiction has a painfully pared vocabulary. Open arbitrarily and you find on one page: feebs-in-overalls; donkeyphuckers; gnoofes; sowskins; ferox-faced oaves; bungpegs; low venereals; pioneeriana. The context here is country. A less rural ambience encourages items like nimptopsical, polypropylene, clapotage and genupectoral. There is a plot as well as words, but this is a sneering concession to such readers as take seriously the blazon A NOVEL on the dust-cover. The hero, who relates to the author through the martyred cleric of the Elizabethan Reform, Théroux d'Arconville, works as English lecturer in an American Southern women's college and falls in love with a student. Marriage is proposed and arranged, but the false hilding falls for another man. Revenge is planned and curses are articulated, but Darconville meets natural death in Venice. This simple tale easily fills 704 pages, for, in the Rabelaisian manner, it is decorated with monstrous catalogues, liturgies, baroque pastiches, diaries — anything, in fact, to prevent the story from moving fast.

Theroux likes to deny his fictional gifts, but they are very much there. The artless dialogue of the students is a great joy, and so is the pornography they read. Let Darconville go to the Wyanoid Baptist Church, and he will hear, for hours, invective like this: "Ain't never been a soul tumblin' through them Gates of Eternity but wadn't first a li'l heap of trash, born in shame, and set on magnetic north to grab at evry pair of glands in sight, pawin' flesh and *doin' like hawgs*!" Chapter LXXXII is twenty pages of unholy litany: "From Eve and her quinces, from Jael the jakesmaid" all the way to "from Marie Duplessis de Camellias", *libera nos, Domine*. A word-drunk book, but one needs an occasional break from fictional sobriety.

The Mosquito Coast

PAUL THEROUX [1981]

The Theroux family is what Ezra Pound would have called a "darned clever bunch" (see *Darconville's Cat*). This novel is clever, superbly composed, also terrifying. Its theme is wholesome enough. Allie Fox, an ingenious American (Yankee really) skilled in the techniques of refrigeration, leaves corrupt and criminal America with his family to start a new and idyllic life in Honduras. Like Robinson Crusoe, he takes into the wilds such fruits of Western technology as will sweeten the Edenic life, and these are chiefly refrigeration. In the jungle he starts to build a gigantic ice-making machine. The project is too vast, it has the seeds of megalomania in it, and Allie Fox's mind begins to totter. The paternalistic sustainer of the good life turns into a kind of fierce Jehovah, one who leads the family towards destruction in the wilderness and is himself destroyed. He is even eaten: "Five birds stood over him — vultures — and they were attacking his head. They made cruel swipes at his scalp.... They held parts of his flesh in their beaks." His family gets back to America: "The world was all right, no better or worse than we had left it — though after what Father had told us, what we saw was like splendour. It was glorious even here, in this old taxi-cab, with the radio playing." Theroux's subject is a fine traditional one — dealt with less expertly and realistically in *The Lord of the Flies*: the dream of the return to innocence always turns into nightmare. The physical impact of the style, the exact observation, the occasional intrusion of the hallucinatory make this a remarkable work of art; its philosophical content is profound.

Creation

GORE VIDAL [1981]

Vidal is a brilliant novelist who shines in a large variety of forms — from the early *Williwaw*, a chronicle of the war at sea written at the age of nineteen, and *The City and the Pillar*, the first serious novel about homosexuality, to the scurrilous satires *Myra Breckenridge* and *Duluth*. *Julian* is a long historical novel, with a painstaking portrait of the emperor who was called the Apostate and a glittering Byzantine background. *Creation* is more ambitious. It deals with the fifth century before Christ, the age of the Persian kings Darius and Xerxes and of Buddha, Confucius, Herodotus, Anaxagoras, Socrates and Pericles. Vidal has said that he wanted to read a novel in which Socrates, Buddha and Confucius all made an appearance: lacking such a book, he had to write it himself.

The narrator-hero is Cyrus Spitama, grandson of the prophet Zoroaster. Brought up in the Persian court he is educated as a soldier along with his friend Xerxes, who is destined to become ruler of the empire which stretches from India to the Mediterranean. Seeking wealth and trade routes for Xerxes, Cyrus meets Buddha in an Indian grove, Confucius by a riverbank in Cathay, Socrates in Athens — a young stonemason who comes to repair the wall of the house where he ends his life. The same questions recur in all the lands that Cyrus visits — how was the universe created and why? Why was evil created as well as good?

It is an incredibly detailed and convincing picture of the ancient world. It is thoughtful as well as witty. It is not, as *Myra Breckenridge* and *Duluth* are, sexually obscene, but it is frank, direct, physical. Vidal has one of the most interesting minds of all living writers, and he engages here the fundamental problems of humanity without allowing modern knowingness to intrude. *Creation* is a genuine recreation of the remote past.

The Rebel Angels

ROBERTSON DAVIES [1982]

I have had to choose between this novel and the same author's more massive *Deptford Trilogy* (*Fifth Business, The Manticore* and *World of Wonders*). *The Rebel Angels* just about wins. The setting of the book is a Canadian university named for St John and the Holy Ghost but called Spook for short. The story embraces the gamut between scatology and eschatology; the former being exemplified in the bequest of John Parlabane, sometime of the Society of the Sacred Mission: "I leave my arsehole, and all necessary integument thereto appertaining, to the Faculty of Philosophy; let it be stretched upon a steel frame so that each New Year's Day the senior professor may blow through it, uttering a rich fruity note, as my salute to the world of which I now take leave, in search of the Great Perhaps." This *grand peut-être* comes from Rabelais, and one of the themes of the novel is an unpublished manuscript of that master, part of the huge untidy Cornish Bequest, greeted with awe and then stolen. *The Rebel Angels* is in the truest sense of the term Rabelaisian, mixing the taste of food and wine and the rapture of physical love with the equally sharp joys of intellectual enquiry. There is theological speculation too — the name of the beautiful heroine Ms Maria Theotoky, meaning "bringer of God", and theology brings in its opposites — blasphemy, heresy, magic, rebel angels.

The most notable disrupter of the rebel angels is Brother Parlabane, lecher, sexual invert, disrupter of order, schismatic. It is against his predatory interest in her Rabelaisian researches that Maria has to fight, along with her frank lust for her professor, another rebel angel named Hollier. But away from the university intrigues, which end in murder and suicide, thrums the bass string of the wisdom of Maria's mother and her uncle Yerko, who are gipsies. They live in an old house which stinks: "a stench all its own pervaded every corner. It was a threnody in the key of Cat major, with ... modulations of old people, waning lives and relinquished hopes." But the gipsy quarters have a life-enhancing richness, expressed in a great Boxing Day dinner at which Maria's mother serves some of Maria's menses in the coffee of Father Darcourt in order that he shall fall in love with her.

The book is about the need to learn balance through the intelligent consultation of law and tradition and the equally intelligent use of the doctrines of the rebel angels. In a word, the novel celebrates humanism. It is a wise, profound and joyful book, Canadian in its feeling of Commonwealth membership, which means that it accepts its European heritage. There is no sexual neurosis in it, as there is in so much fiction of the United States. Its vivacity is proper to a nation whose future still lies all before it. Robertson Davies is without doubt Nobel Prize material.

Ancient Evenings

NORMAN MAILER [1983]

There is one ancient evening in particular, spent 3000 years ago at the court of Rameses IX. It is the Night of the Pig, a rare occasion for the violating of taboos and speaking out freely: even Isis, Osiris and Horus may be mocked. Presiding over a select dinner party is the Pharaoh himself; his guests are Menenhetet I, an old man of great experience in war, policy and magic, Menenhetet's grand-daughter, the beautiful and devious Hathfertiti, and her husband and son. The husband, a somewhat dim and timorous personage, is the Overseer of the Royal Cosmetic Box: the Pharaoh's maquillage is a reflection of, and an influence on, the condition of the Egypt he rules. The son, who is only six, is Menenhetet II, and he dies and is mummified before the novel properly starts. We meet him in the prologue in the person of his Ka, one of his seven doubles or shadows, and it is his Ka that is remembering this ancient evening in great detail.

Rameses IX is a charming man but not a good monarch. He is aware of a fatal inability to control the state: there is corruption in the ministries, and there is even a workers' strike caused by failure to deliver their corn supplies. His worthlessness as a ruler will be shown up by the failure of the Nile to flood. On this night of plain speaking he demands to know from old Menenhetet something of the secret of the strength of his ancestor Rameses II whom, in a former life 180 years before, Menenhetet served as a charioteer, an army general and governor of the harem. Menenhetet tells all: it takes him nearly seven hundred pages.

The secret of power lies in magic, and magic is essentially control of the lower human functions. In a word, magic is anal. You sodomize the enemy to probe the caves of his strength. Rameses IX sees Egypt as looking like a crack between the globes of the buttocks. Egypt is fertile because of Nile mud, and mud is a form of faeces. Old Menenhetet has, to the shock of the court, eaten bat-droppings in order to learn magic. Khepera, that greatest of the gods, is a dung-beetle; the Land of the Dead is his, and in it you must face the worst of faecal orders in order to achieve a passage to the next life. The arse of the Pharaoh excretes magical droppings into a sacred golden bowl. The source of power is to be found in anal sorcery.

This novel is perhaps the best reconstruction of the far past since Flaubert's *Salammbô*, but Mailer's eye is on the modern age, especially the psychic problems of America. These problems may find a solution through an understanding of the repressed areas of human sexuality, with the reality of magic. Our own rationality has failed. Here, he seems to say, is a complex civilization of high achievement based on the irrational, on the radial power of a magic whose centre is both decay and resurrection. This is a different book, on whose writing and research Mailer spent over ten years, but it is not only about magic, it is magical in itself. If *The Naked and the Dead* remains his best work, this runs it very close.

BIBLIOGRAPHY

This bibliography has been compiled by the Publishers. Date of first publication and original publisher in both England and America have been obtained from the British Library catalogue and the National Union catalogue in the British Museum Reading Room. The dates have been cross-checked against the Whitaker and Bowker Cumulative Lists. The country of original publication is given first.

The information about current availability of the titles has been obtained from Whitaker's *Book in Print* on microfiche and Bowker's *Books in Print 1983-84.* As titles move regularly in and out of print the information is of necessity a picture of a situation which is constantly changing.

The Publishers would welcome any corrections if there are errors in this bibliography.

ACHEBE, CHINUA

A Man of the People

London: Heinemann, 1966
New York: John Day, 1966
Current editions:
UK: Heinemann
USA: Doubleday Anchor

ALDISS, BRIAN

Life in the West

London: Weidenfeld & Nicolson, 1980
New York: no edition
Current editions:
UK: Corgi

AMIS, KINGSLEY

Lucky Jim

London: Gollancz, 1954 (copyright 1953)
New York: Doubleday, 1954
Current editions
UK: Gollancz and Penguin
USA: Penguin

AMIS, KINGSLEY
The Anti-Death League
London: Gollancz, 1966
New York: Harcourt Brace, 1966
Current editions:
UK: Gollancz and Penguin
USA: out of print

BALDWIN, JAMES
Another Country
New York: Dial Press, 1962
London: Michael Joseph, 1963
Current editions:
UK: Michael Joseph and Corgi
USA: out of print

BALLARD, J.G.
The Unlimited Dream Company
London: Jonathan Cape, 1979
New York: Holt, Rinehart & Winston, 1979
Current editions:
UK: Cape and Panther/Granada
USA: out of print

BARTH, JOHN
Giles Goat-boy
New York: Doubleday, 1966
London: Secker & Warburg, 1967
Current editions:
UK: Panther/Granada
USA: Doubleday, Bantam and Fawcett

BELLOW, SAUL
The Victim
New York: Vanguard Press, 1947
London: John Lehmann, 1948
Current editions:
UK: Penguin
USA: Vanguard, NAL and Avon

BELLOW, SAUL
Humboldt's Gift
New York: Viking Press, 1975

London: Secker & Warburg, 1975
Current editions:
UK: Secker and Penguin
USA: Viking and Avon

BOWEN, ELIZABETH
The Heat of the Day
London: Jonathan Cape, 1949
New York: Knopf, 1949 (copyright 1948)
Current editions:
UK: Cape and Penguin
USA: Buccaneer and Avon

BRADBURY, MALCOLM
The History Man
London: Secker & Warburg, 1975
New York: Houghton Mifflin, 1976
Current editions:
UK: Secker and Arrow
USA: out of print

BRAINE, JOHN
Room at the Top
London: Eyre & Spottiswoode, 1957
Boston: Houghton Mifflin, 1957
Current editions:
UK: Eyre & Spottiswoode and Magnum
USA: Methuen Inc

CARY, JOYCE
The Horse's Mouth
London: Michael Joseph, 1944
New York: Harper & Row, 1944
Current editions:
UK: Penguin
USA: Harper

CHANDLER, RAYMOND
The Long Goodbye
London: Hamish Hamilton, 1953
Boston: Houghton Mifflin, 1954
Current editions:
UK: Picador
USA: Ballantine

COMPTON-BURNETT, IVY

The Mighty and Their Fall

London: Gollancz, 1961

New York: Simon & Schuster, 1962

Current editions:

UK: Gollancz

USA: David and Charles Inc

COOPER, WILLIAM

Scenes from Provincial Life

London: Jonathan Cape, 1950

New York: Scribner, 1967 (as *Scenes from Life* and including *Scenes from Married Life*)

Current editions:

UK: Macmillan and Methuen

USA: Dutton

DAVIES, ROBERTSON

The Rebel Angels

Toronto: Macmillan, 1982

New York: Viking Press, 1982

London: Allen Lane, 1982

Current editions:

UK: Allen Lane and Penguin

USA: Viking and Penguin

DEIGHTON, LEN

Bomber

London: Jonathan Cape, 1970

New York: Harper & Row, 1970

Current editions:

UK: Panther/Granada

USA: out of print

DURRELL, LAWRENCE

The Alexandria Quartet:

Justine

London: Faber & Faber, 1957

New York: Dutton, 1957

Balthazar

London: Faber & Faber, 1958

New York: Dutton, 1958

Mountolive

London: Faber & Faber, 1958

New York: Dutton, 1959

Clea

London: Faber & Faber, 1960

New York: Dutton, 1960

Current editions:

UK: Faber

USA: Dutton and WSP

ELLISON, RALPH

Invisible Man

New York: Random House, 1952

London: Gollancz, 1953

Current editions:

UK: Penguin

USA: Random, Modern Library and Vintage

FAULKNER, WILLIAM

The Mansion

New York: Random House, 1959

London: Chatto & Windus, 1961

Current editions:

UK: Chatto

USA: Random House,

FLEMING, IAN

Goldfinger

London: Jonathan Cape, 1959

New York: Macmillan, 1959

Current editions:

UK: Cape and Panther/Granada

USA: French & European and Berkley

FOWLES, JOHN

The French Lieutenant's Woman

London: Jonathan Cape, 1969

Boston: Little Brown, 1969

Current editions:

UK: Cape and Panther/Granada

USA: Little Brown and NAL

FRAYN, MICHAEL

Sweet Dreams

London: Collins, 1973

New York: Viking Press, 1974

Current editions:
UK: Fontana
USA: out of print

GOLDING, WILLIAM
The Spire
London: Faber & Faber, 1964
New York: Harcourt Brace, 1965
Current editions:
UK: Faber
USA: out of print

GORDIMER, NADINE
The Late Bourgeois World
London: Gollancz, 1966
New York: Viking Press, 1966
Current editions:
UK: Cape and Penguin
USA: Penguin

GRAY, ALASDAIR
Lanark: A Life in Four Books
Edinburgh: Canongate, 1981
New York: Harper & Row, 1982
Current editions:
UK: Panther/Granada
USA: out of print

GREEN, HENRY
Party Going
London: Hogarth Press, 1939
Toronto: Longman, 1939
Current editions:
UK: Picador
USA: Kelley

GREENE, GRAHAM
The Power and the Glory
London: Heinemann, 1940
New York: Viking Press, 1940 (as *The Labyrinthine Ways*)
Current editions:
UK: Bodley Head/Heinemann and Penguin
USA: Viking and Penguin

GREENE, GRAHAM

The Heart of the Matter

London: Heinemann, 1948
New York: Viking Press, 1948
Current editions:
UK: Bodley Head/Heinemann and Penguin
USA: Viking and Penguin

HARRIS, WILSON

Heartland

London: Faber & Faber, 1964
New York: No edition
Current editions:
UK: out of print

HARTLEY, L.P.

Facial Justice

London: Hamish Hamilton, 1960
New York: Doubleday, 1961
Current editions:
UK: out of print
USA: out of print

HELLER, JOSEPH

Catch-22

New York: Simon & Schuster, 1961
London: Jonathan Cape, 1962
Current editions:
UK: Cape and Corgi
USA: Simon & Schuster, Dell and Modern Library

HEMINGWAY, ERNEST

For Whom the Bell Tolls

New York: Scribner, 1940
London: Jonathan Cape, 1941
Current editions:
UK: Cape and Panther/Granada
USA: Scribner

HEMINGWAY, ERNEST

The Old Man and the Sea

New York: Scribner, 1952
London: Jonathan Cape, 1952

Current editions:
UK: Cape and Panther/Granada
USA: Scribner

HOBAN, RUSSELL
Riddley Walker
London: Jonathan Cape, 1980
New York: Summit Books, 1980
Current editions:
UK: Picador
USA: Summit and WSP

HUGHES, RICHARD
The Fox in the Attic
London: Chatto & Windus, 1961
New York: Harper & Row, 1961
Current editions:
UK: Chatto and Panther/Granada
USA: Harper

HUXLEY, ALDOUS
After Many a Summer
London: Chatto & Windus, 1939
New York: Harper, 1939 (as *After Many a Summer Dies the Swan*)
Current editions:
UK: Panther/Granada
USA: River City Press

HUXLEY, ALDOUS
Ape and Essence
New York: Harper, 1948
London: Chatto & Windus, 1949
Current editions:
UK: Chatto and Granada
USA: out of print

HUXLEY, ALDOUS
Island
London: Chatto & Windus, 1962
New York: Harper & Row, 1962
Current editions:
UK: Chatto and Panther/Granada
USA: Harper

ISHERWOOD, CHRISTOPHER

A Single Man

New York: Simon & Schuster, 1964
London: Methuen, 1964
Current editions:
UK: Methuen and Magnum
USA: Avon

JOHNSON, PAMELA HANSFORD

An Error of Judgement

London: Macmillan, 1962
New York: Harcourt Brace, 1962
Current editions:
UK: out of print
USA: out of print

JONG, ERICA

How to Save Your Own Life

New York: Holt, Rinehart & Winston, 1977
London: Secker & Warburg, 1977
Current editions:
UK: Secker and Panther/Granada
USA: NAL

JOYCE, JAMES

Finnegans Wake

London: Faber & Faber, 1939
New York: Viking Press, 1939
Current editions:
UK: Faber
USA: Viking and Penguin

LESSING, DORIS

The Golden Notebook

London: Michael Joseph, 1962
New York: Simon & Schuster, 1962
Current editions:
UK: Michael Joseph and Panther/Granada
USA: Bantam

LODGE, DAVID

How Far Can You Go?

London: Secker & Warburg, 1980
New York: Morrow, 1982

Current editions:
UK: Secker and Penguin
USA: out of print

LOWRY, MALCOLM
Under the Volcano
London: Jonathan Cape, 1947
New York: Reynal & Hitchcock, 1947
Current editions:
UK: Penguin
USA: Harper and NAL

McCARTHY, MARY
The Groves of Academe
New York: Harcourt Brace, 1952
London: Heinemann, 1953
Current editions:
UK: out of print
USA: Harcourt Brace and Avon

MACINNES, COLIN
The London Novels:
City of Spades
London: MacGibbon & Kee, 1957
New York: Macmillan, 1958
Absolute Beginners
London: MacGibbon & Kee, 1959
New York: Macmillan, 1960
Mr Love and Justice
London: MacGibbon & Kee, 1960
New York: Dutton, 1961
Current editions:
UK: Allison & Busby
USA: Allison & Busby/Schocken

MAILER, NORMAN
The Naked and the Dead
New York: Holt, Rinehart & Winston, 1948
London: Allan Wingate, 1949
Current editions:
UK: Deutsch and Panther/Granada
USA: Holt, Rinehart and NAL

MAILER, NORMAN

Ancient Evenings

Boston: Little Brown, 1983
London: Macmillan, 1983
Current editions:
UK: Macmillan
USA: Little Brown

MALAMUD, BERNARD

The Assistant

New York: Farrar, Straus & Cudahy, 1957
London: Eyre & Spottiswoode, 1959
Current editions:
UK: Chatto
USA: Farrar Straus and Avon

MALAMUD, BERNARD

Dubin's Lives

New York: Farrar, Straus & Giroux, 1979
London: Chatto & Windus, 1979
Current editions:
UK: Chatto and Penguin
USA: Farrar Straus and Avon

MANNING, OLIVIA

The Balkan Trilogy:

Great Fortune

London: Heinemann, 1960
New York: Doubleday, 1961

The Spoilt City

London: Heinemann, 1962
New York: Doubleday, 1962

Friends and Heroes

London: Heinemann, 1965
New York: Doubleday, 1966
Current editions:
UK: Heinemann and Penguin
USA: Penguin

MAUGHAM, SOMERSET

The Razor's Edge

London: Heinemann, 1944
New York: Doubleday, Doran, 1944

Current editions:
UK: Heinemann and Pan
USA: Ayer and Penguin

MOORE, BRIAN
The Doctor's Wife
London: Jonathan Cape, 1976
New York: Farrar, Straus & Giroux, 1976
Current editions:
UK: Cape and Corgi
USA: Farrar Straus

MURDOCH, IRIS
The Bell
London: Chatto & Windus, 1958
New York: Viking Press, 1958
Current editions:
UK: Panther/Granada
USA: out of print

NABOKOV, VLADIMIR
Pale Fire
New York: Putnam, 1962
London: Widenfeld & Nicolson, 1962
Current editions:
UK: Penguin
USA: Putnam and Berkley

NABOKOV, VLADIMIR
The Defense
New York: Putnam, 1964
London: Weidenfeld & Nicolson, 1964 (as *The Defence*)
Current editions:
UK: out of print
USA: out of print

NAIPAUL, V.S.
A Bend in the River
London: André Deutsch, 1979
New York: Knopf, 1979
Current editions:
UK: Deutsch and Penguin
USA: Knopf and Random

NARAYAN R.K.
The Vendor of Sweets
London: Bodley Head, 1967 (as *The Sweet-vendor*)
New York: Avon, 1971
Current editions:
UK: Penguin
USA: Penguin

NYE, ROBERT
Falstaff
London: Hamish Hamilton, 1976
Boston: Little Brown, 1976
Current editions:
UK: Hamish Hamilton and Penguin
USA: out of print

O'BRIEN, FLANN
At Swim-Two-Birds
London: Longman, 1939
New York: Pantheon, 1951
Current editions:
UK: Hart Davis and Penguin
USA: NAL

O'CONNOR, FLANNERY
Wise Blood
New York: Harcourt Brace, 1952
London: Neville Spearman, 1955
Current editions:
UK: Faber
USA: Farrar Straus

O'HARA, JOHN
The Lockwood Concern
New York: Random House, 1965
London: Hodder & Stoughton, 1966
Current editions:
UK: out of print
USA: out of print

ORWELL, GEORGE
Nineteen Eighty-four
London: Secker & Warburg, 1949

New York: Harcourt Brace, 1949
Current editions:
UK: Secker and Penguin
USA: Harcourt Brace, Buccaneer and NAL

PEAKE, MERVYN
Titus Groan
London: Eyre & Spottiswoode, 1946
New York: Reynal & Hitchcock, 1946
Current editions:
UK: Penguin
USA: Overlook Press

PERCY, WALKER
The Last Gentleman
New York: Farrar, Straus & Giroux, 1966
London: Eyre & Spottiswoode, 1967
Current editions:
UK: Secker
USA: Farrar Straus

PLUNKETT, JAMES
Farewell Companions
London: Hutchinson, 1977
New York: Coward McCann, 1977
Current editions:
UK: Hutchinson and Arrow
USA: out of print

POWELL, ANTHONY
A Dance to the Music of Time:
A Question of Upbringing
London: Heinemann, 1951
New York: Scribner, 1951
A Buyer's Market
London: Heinemann, 1952
New York: Scribner, 1953
The Acceptance World
London: Heinemann, 1955
New York: Farrar, Straus & Giroux, 1956
At Lady Molly's
London: Heinemann, 1957
Boston: Little Brown, 1958

Casanova's Chinese Restaurant
London: Heinemann, 1960
Boston: Little Brown, 1960
The Kindly Ones
London: Heinemann, 1962
Boston: Little Brown, 1962
The Valley of Bones
London: Heinemann, 1964
Boston: Little Brown, 1964
The Soldier's Art
London: Heinemann, 1966
Boston: Little Brown, 1966
The Military Philosophers
London: Heinemann, 1968
Boston: Little Brown, 1969
Books Do Furnish a Room
London: Heinemann, 1971
Boston: Little Brown 1971
Temporary Kings
London: Heinemann, 1973
Boston: Little Brown, 1973
Hearing Secret Harmonies
London: Heinemann, 1975
Boston: Little Brown, 1975
Current editions:
UK: Heinemann, Fontana and Flamingo
USA: Little Brown and Popular Library

PRIESTLEY, J.B.
The Image Men
London: Heinemann, 1968
Boston: Little Brown, 1969
Current editions:
UK: Heinemann
USA: out of print

PYNCHON, THOMAS
Gravity's Rainbow
New York: Viking Press, 1973
London: Jonathan Cape, 1973
Current editions:
UK: Picador
USA: Viking, Bantam and Penguin

RICHLER, MORDECAI

Cocksure

Toronto: McClelland & Stewart, 1968
New York: Simon & Schuster, 1968
London: Weidenfeld & Nicolson, 1968
Current editions:
UK: Panther/Granada
USA: out of print

ROBERTS, KEITH

Pavane

London: Hart Davis, 1968
New York: Doubleday, 1968
Current editions:
UK: out of print
USA: Ace Books

ROTH, PHILIP

Portnoy's Complaint

New York: Random House, 1969
London: Jonathan Cape, 1969
Current editions:
UK: Cape and Corgi
USA: Random, Modern Library and Bantam

SALINGER, J.D.

The Catcher in the Rye

Boston: Little Brown, 1951
London: Hamish Hamilton, 1951
Current editions:
UK: Hamish Hamilton and Penguin
USA: Little Brown and Bantam

SANSOM, WILLIAM

The Body

London: Hogarth Press, 1949
New York: Harcourt Brace, 1949
Current editions:
UK: out of print
USA: out of print

SCHULBERG, BUDD

The Disenchanted

New York: Random House, 1950

London: Bodley Head, 1951
Current editions:
UK: Allison & Busby
USA: out of print

SCOTT, PAUL
Staying On
London: Heinemann, 1977
New York: Morrow, 1977
Current editions:
UK: Heinemann and Panther/Granada
USA: Morrow and Avon

SHUTE, NEVIL
No Highway
London: Heinemann, 1948
New York: Morrow, 1948
Current editions:
UK: Heinemann and Pan
USA: out of print

SILLITOE, ALAN
Saturday Night and Sunday Morning
London: W.H. Allen, 1958
New York: Knopf, 1958
Current editions:
UK: W.H. Allen and Star
USA: Knopf and NAL

SNOW, C.P.
Strangers and Brothers:
Time of Hope
London: Macmillan, 1949
New York: Macmillan, 1950
George Passant (as *Strangers and Brothers*)
London: Macmillan, 1940
New York: Scribner, 1960
The Conscience of the Rich
London: Macmillan, 1958
New York: Scribner, 1958
The Light and the Dark
London: Faber & Faber, 1947
New York: Macmillan, 1948

The Masters
London: Macmillan. 1951
New York: Macmillan, 1951
The New Men
London: Macmillan, 1954
New York: Scribner, 1954
Homecomings
London: Macmillan, 1956
New York: Scribner, 1956 (as *The Homecoming*)
The Affair
London: Macmillan, 1960
New York: Scribner, 1960
Corridors of Power
London: Macmillan, 1964
New York: Scribner, 1964
The Sleep of Reason
London: Macmillan, 1968
New York: Scribner, 1969
Last Things
London: Macmillan, 1970
New York: Scribner, 1970
Current editions:
UK: Macmillan and Penguin
USA: Scribner

SPARK, MURIEL
The Girls of Slender Means
London: Macmillan, 1963
New York: Knopf, 1963
Current editions:
UK: Macmillan and Penguin
USA: out of print

SPARK, MURIEL
The Mandelbaum Gate
London: Macmillan, 1965
New York: Knopf, 1965
Current editions:
UK: Macmillan and Penguin
USA: Putnam

STYRON, WILLIAM

Sophie's Choice

New York: Random House, 1979
London: Jonathan Cape, 1979
Current editions:
UK: Cape and Corgi
USA: Random and Bantam

THEROUX, ALEXANDER

Darconville's Cat

New York: Doubleday, 1981
London: Hamish Hamilton, 1983
Current editions:
UK: Hamish Hamilton
USA: Doubleday

THEROUX, PAUL

The Mosquito Coast

London: Hamish Hamilton, 1981
New York: Houghton Mifflin
Current editions:
UK: Hamish Hamilton and Penguin
USA: Houghton Mifflin and Avon

TOOLE, JOHN KENNEDY

A Confederacy of Dunces

Louisiana: Louisiana State University Press, 1980
London: Allen Lane, 1981
Current editions:
UK: Allen Lane and Penguin
USA: Louisiana University Press and Grove

UPDIKE, JOHN

The Coup

New York: Knopf, 1978
London: Deutsch, 1979
Current editions:
UK: Deutsch and Penguin
USA· Knopf and Fawcett

VIDAL, GORE

Creation

New York: Random House, 1981
London: Heinemann, 1981
Current editions:
UK: Heinemann and Panther/Granada
USA: Random and Ballantine

WARNER, REX

The Aerodrome

London: John Lane, 1941
Philadelphia: J.B. Lippincott, 1941
Current editions:
UK: Bodley Head and Oxford University Press
USA: Oxford University Press

WAUGH, EVELYN

Brideshead Revisited

London: Chapman & Hall, 1945
Boston: Little Brown, 1945
Current editions:
London: Methuen and Penguin
New York: Little Brown

WAUGH, EVELYN

The Sword of Honour

Men at Arms

London: Chapman & Hall, 1952
Boston: Little Brown, 1952

Officers and Gentlemen

London: Chapman & Hall, 1955
Boston: Little Brown, 1955

Unconditional Surrender

London: Chapman & Hall, 1961
Boston: Little Brown, 1961 (as *The End of the Battle*)
Current editions:
UK: Penguin
USA: Little Brown and G.K. Hall

WHITE, PATRICK
Riders in the Chariot
New York: Viking Press, 1961
London: Eyre & Spottiswoode, 1961
Current editions:
UK: Cape and Penguin
USA: Viking

WHITE, T.H.
The Once and Future King
London: Collins, 1958
New York: Putnam, 1958
Current editions:
UK: Collins
USA: Berkley

WILLIAMSON, HENRY
A Chronicle of Ancient Sunlight:
The Dark Lantern
London: Macdonald, 1951
New York: no edition
Donkey Boy
London: Macdonald, 1952
New York: no edition
Young Philip Maddison
London: Macdonald, 1953
New York: no edition
How Dear is Life
London: Macdonald, 1954
New York: no edition
A Fox under My Cloak
London: Macdonald, 1955
New York: no edition
The Golden Virgin
London: Macdonald, 1957
New York: no edition
Love and the Loveless
London: Macdonald, 1958
New York: no edition

A Test to Destruction
London: Macdonald, 1960
New York: no edition
The Innocent Moon
London: Macdonald, 1961
New York: no edition
It Was the Nightingale
London: Macdonald, 1962
New York: no edition
The Power of the Dead
London: Macdonald, 1963
New York: no edition
The Phoenix Generation
London: Macdonald, 1965
New York: no edition
A Solitary War
London: Macdonald, 1966
New York: no edition
Lucifer Before Sunrise
London: Macdonald, 1967
New York: no edition
The Gale of the World
London: Macdonald, 1969
New York: no edition
Current editions:
UK: *A Fox under my Cloak*, Chivers, remainder of sequence out of print.

WILSON, ANGUS
The Old Men at the Zoo
London: Secker & Warburg, 1961
New York: Viking Press, 1961
Current editions:
UK: Panther/Granada
USA: out of print

WILSON, ANGUS
Late Call
London: Secker & Warburg, 1964
New York: Viking Press, 1965
Current editions:
UK: Penguin and Granada/Panther
USA: out of print

WOUK, HERMAN

The Caine Mutiny

New York: Doubleday, 1951
London: Jonathan Cape, 1951
Current editions:
UK: out of print
USA: Doubleday and Pocket Books

INDEX

(Bold page numbers refer to book choice entries)